A Defence of Masochism

Sadomasochism has been the sexual phenomenon of the nineties. We all seem to know what sadism is, but masochism is more complicated and more elusive. Who are the masochists, and why are they doing it? Is it a dangerous perversion or a harmless, playful pastime? How deep is its grip on the imagination, and how far-reaching? Are women more masochistic than men, or is it the other way round? And why, as any masochist will tell you, is a good sadist so hard to find?

A Defence of Masochism draws on a wide range of literary, psychoanalytic and cultural sources, from Sacher-Masoch's *Venus in Furs* to David Lynch films and *The Story of O*. Anita Phillips suggests that masochism is not only a universal trait – which Freud came close to recognizing – but also a crucial component in our capacity to fantasize and imagine, from infancy into adulthood. She takes issue with aspects of feminism and psychoanalysis, and introduces controversial ideas about perversion and perversity which challenge the legacy of traditional sexology. What emerges is a fresh and striking picture of human longing, curiosity and eroticism.

Elegantly written and highly engaging, this lively, polemical book touches a raw nerve in contemporary culture.

Anita Phillips writes essays on contemporary sexuality and art, as well as literary fiction. She has worked for some years as a freelance editor, while working on collaborative projects with artists and writing her first novel. *The Virtues, the Vices and All the Passions* was published by Polygon in 1991. She has a doctorate from Queen Mary College, London, and lectures widely both in academic and art contexts. She co-edits a literary journal, *interstice*, and has published numerous articles and short stories.

A Defence of Masochism

ANITA PHILLIPS

faber and faber

First published in 1998
by Faber and Faber Ltd
3 Queen Square London WC1N 3AU
This paperback edition first published in 1999

Typeset by Faber and Faber Ltd
Printed in England by Mackays of Chatham plc, Chatham, Kent

A CIP record for this book
is available from the British Library

ISBN 0-571-19697-7

10 9 8 7 6 5 4 3 2 1

For my mother and father

Contents

Acknowledgements

Malcolm Bowie: for being the one who can be respected.

Stephen Barber: for his generous encouragement.

Michael Worton: for his integrity.

Helen Hayward: for extraordinary insight, scepticism and lucidity.

Julian Loose: for ruthless exigence.

Patrick ffrench: for applying his theoretical, imaginative and speculative virtuosity to the task of making life attain to the condition of art.

Introduction

The party was nearly over. A sandy-haired young Scottish lawyer approached me, having heard I was writing a book on masochism. Tipsy and mesmerized by the idea, he told me that he believed women were all masochists and men sadists. It was a fact that nobody admitted, it was covered up, and he really wanted to talk about it to me – the only other person in the world to have discovered (he seemed to think) this undeniable, essential truth. Finally his friends, laughing, pulled him away.

In a café near Regent's Park one afternoon I met a close friend from academia who looks like a boyish version of Nicole Kidman. We had both finished our doctorates at around the same time, but now, she told me, she was having difficulty in applying for jobs. The reason was her 'inherent masochism'. She smiled wryly, as if in some discomfort.

These are just two examples of the widely different meanings people attribute to the term, and the widely differing ways they relate their experience to it. In the ensuing discussion with my friend, I aired my suspicion that she was over-keen to detect a masochistic origin in her difficulties. Surely they could be attributed to understandable post-thesis emotional reactions, such as ambivalence and self-doubt? In my brief, joky exchange with the lawyer, I tried to challenge what I considered his over-simplified views by saying that masochism as a term had been invented to describe not a female, but a male sexual tendency.

One of the aims of this book is to understand what kinds of things really are masochistic and what should be left aside and reconsidered in a different light. Masochism has become a convenient catch-all word, and is used to cover a multitude of sins as well as graces. I would say that misunderstanding of masochistic behaviour is widespread, and the reasons for this are predominantly historical. Over the course of time, with gradual changes of use, theoretical redefinitions and reappropriations, meanings have become obscured. This is confusing for everybody.

My premise is that our picture of masochism is wildly skewed. In this book I stand up for masochism. If that sounds an unlikely project it is because of a vague and utterly mistaken belief that masochists enjoy and absorb violence, including intellectual violence. On the contrary, masochism flees violence and constructs an unusual and compelling scenario that needs to be understood in order to work. It is a very intelligent perversion.

This project involves rescuing masochism from the clinical discourses that named it and endowed it with its identity as a sickness, as something pathological, and setting it back into the context of diverse human experience and artistic creativity from which it was first plucked. I want this to be an encouraging, enlivening kind of book, rather than a purely analytical treatise which attempts to establish norms of behaviour.

Because nobody knows exactly what masochism means, many people misunderstand their own behaviour and may interpret their desires and actions clumsily and anxiously. For example, the lawyer at the party seemed to be hoping that I would confirm his suggestion that all women like to be dominated, perhaps to relieve his guilt about enjoying the dominant role. Fears of effeminacy may also play a part. Many men disown inadmissible longings for submission, which threaten their sense of masculinity, by handing them over, making them the sole property of the opposite sex. In this book I argue that there is nothing emasculating about male masochism, nor anything unethical about male sexual domination (except in the case of forced sex or rape, which transgresses the delicate contract between sexual partners).

My academic friend describes herself as masochistic for altogether different reasons, though I think guilt comes into the picture here, too. She can afford and would like to extend herself as a writer on literature and human experience, but she has not yet quite built up her confidence and sense of autonomy. Masochism, conceived of negatively, can be used as a self-punishing word, a way of being hard on yourself when you don't come up to your own standards. And my friend has very high standards indeed. But masochism is not only about pain; it is one of the roads to intense pleasure and renewal. Sexual masochism offers a way through for people who push themselves too hard, who overachieve, who are never good enough; it gives an alternative to the impossible advice to take it easy. I want to demonstrate how psychologically healing sexual pain can be, in transforming inner trouble into something that your body can take and survive.

Here are some examples of other kinds of things that people think are masochistic, all volunteered to me during the hundreds of conversations on the subject that have occurred spontaneously in a range of contexts (for example, around the dinner table, at a student seminar, in intimate conversation with a close friend) since I began my research. Which of these is genuinely masochistic?

- Running the London Marathon
- Enjoying the fantasy of being raped by a fascist
- Eating a vindaloo in an Indian restaurant, a dish so hot for your palate that you would break out in a sweat all over your body, yet still feel drawn to repeat the experience every few weeks
- Doing a Ph.D. (this example came from several sources)
- Being so sensitive that you are always feeling crushed by the strength of other people's will
- Having your chest stepped on by a woman in stilettos so

    that the heels press down upon your nipples
- Being passionately in love with somebody who doesn't know you exist
- Swimming in the English Channel in late November
- Imagining what it would be like to make love with a Sumo wrestler, from underneath.

By bringing masochism into focus I hope to prevent it being used as a kind of emotional and sexual waste-basket, a receptacle for the odds and ends of people's behaviour, for the things they cannot explain about themselves but still feel strongly. Removing the waste-basket should mean that those issues can be examined on their own terms. Certainly the blame (or glory) should no longer be laid at masochism's door. Masochism should not be too quickly disowned, as in the case of the lawyer, nor too easily owned, as in the academic's.

In this book, I want to stress two important principles. The first is that masochism is not about what people do on their own; it is something that has to involve another person, even if the other person is only there in the imagination. The marathon runner, the swimmer, the curry addict and the labouring, impoverished postgraduate can be excluded right from the start. All except the third do have something in common with masochists, and that is their asceticism, a subject that I will return to. But masochism is always centrally about some form of desire or feeling in relation to another person.

The second point is about sex. I think there is a form of masochism involved in art, but fundamentally, masochism is a sexual matter. Rape fantasies, unrequited love, desires for Sumo wrestlers or for spiked heels would all be included. A kind of voluntary hypersensitivity would be, too, as an extension of sexual behaviour into a general realm of social interaction.

I hope that readers of this book will gain a better idea of what masochism consists of, how and why they are masochis-

tic in their own particular ways. They may feel relieved or per-
turbed. I would like them to come away feeling they have
more insight into themselves than before, and are more able to
handle the challenge of sexuality. People occasionally ask me,
'Are you a masochist, then?' I always answer that I am, but the
question is irritating. It is as if they want to label me as belong-
ing to some rare species, the kind that get crept up on by television cameras wanting to film bizarre courtship rituals for the
delectation of nature lovers all over the country. I am not a
masochist when I am doing the ironing or having lunch with a
friend; it is not something that defines who I am, that gives me
an identity. It is not that totalitarian.

Enjoying, for example, being sexually dominated does not
preclude you from also enjoying being on top. Or, for that
matter, from taking pleasure in all kinds of other sexual possibilities. Masochism may be something you want to do at a particular time in your life for particular reasons, you may get
what you want from it and move on. It can be part of a highly
varied sexual life, something that is part of a range of options,
or the preferred one. Or it can be an imaginative possibility, a
springboard for artistic and spiritual engagement. The idea
that some people can be defined as masochists does not quite
indicate how things work. Masochism requires a different perspective from, say, homosexuality, which gay people tend to
feel is a permanent, explicit feature and an important source of
identity. We are all masochists – at least some of the time, in
some form or other, because in an important way, the sense of
a self depends on it. ('If I can be invaded, or imagine it happening to me, I must exist.')

With the advent of sexology towards the end of the last century, a language of sexuality and perversion was tortured,
coerced into existence. This forced (but not masochistic)
speech has come down to us, has found its way into popular
understanding of sexual life, so that instead of simply enjoying

this or getting pleasure from that, we impute to ourselves this 'behaviour' or that 'tendency'. If people believe the sexologists about what is normal and what abnormal, they are likely either to conform and lead disastrously drab lives, especially when it comes to sex, or to carry on in a furtive or rebellious way. None of this is necessary. You do not have to stick to the missionary position once a week on a Saturday night, nor, on the other hand, go for the whole nipple-piercing, bondage and S/M subculture. There are plenty of options in between.

Masochism is a fairly young word. That is to say that before the late nineteenth century, there was no word for the multiplicitous desires and acts that now are grouped together within it. Putting a name to something involves all kinds of separations, reconstructions, redefinitions, uprootings from context. The naming of masochism came about unsympathetically, clumsily, and for the writer whose name was appropriated, damagingly. This is one of the reasons for the mixture of recognition and confusion that the term tends to evoke.

'Masochism' denotes a disorder discovered or formulated by a nineteenth-century sexologist, Baron Dr Richard von Krafft-Ebing: it is just over a century old, as a clinical concept, having been around since 1890, or 1892 in the English-speaking world. There are no alternative names for it in current use, though there was an early clinical term 'algolagnia', meaning the desire for pain, and a word with vastly different connotations in Sacher-Masoch's novels, 'supersensuality'. Neither of these has survived. This paucity of terminology is something which in itself deserves attention. Unlike the clinical term 'invert', which has been used to designate homosexuals, no other obvious vocabulary can be reclaimed, no equivalents of the more elevated 'Sapphic', meaning lesbian, or the more street-level 'queer', meaning gay. Perhaps this is because no historical counter-culture has consistently celebrated masochistic pleasure (there is no Masochists' Liberation Front, and one can see why). Nor have whole societies been organized along explicitly masochistic principles, as in the case of the ancient Greeks with homosexuality. Masochism as a term has an invented, ersatz feel about it. It has signally failed to defend itself as a human tendency, resisting reclamation, generalization, the movements of empowerment and integration that have transformed and enlarged views across the century; it has so far stood outside these liberating surges, either refusing or being unable to reveal itself as an authentic mode of experience.

A century after Krafft-Ebing, masochism is still defined as a perversion, and masochists share their dubious distinction with a mixed bag of companions, from necrophiliacs to beast fetishists. For this reason alone, if one day you discover your masochistic tendencies, or have them gently but firmly pointed out by well-meaning friends, it is likely to be a bit of a shock. You have slipped over on to the wrong side of the tracks, and you may begin to investigate all your major life decisions in a new light. Did you make a serious professional mistake because of your masochistic tendencies? Do you keep falling in love with the wrong people because of it? Would your life be more successful, more healthy, if you stopped indulging in those perverse thoughts and acts?

The answer to all of these questions is, probably, no. There are all sorts of good reasons for doing things that seem wrong superficially. For example, falling in love with the wrong person may be something you do because you are not ready to settle down, but you do like to feel passionate about somebody. The major professional mistake may be the own goal that puts a change of job on the cards, which you secretly wanted but wouldn't have had the nerve to accomplish directly. And as for success, it is not everyone's goal, especially if it means giving up your fantasy life.

Suppose, on the other hand, you decide to live with your own quirks and complexities. If you really are actively masochistic (given the massive levels of misunderstanding, there's a good chance your friend is wrong), it may be that there is no alternative to continuing as you have begun. And after a while you might begin to feel entitled to a little harmless perversion. You might even start to question why something that was perfectly respectable for Shakespeare (that 'lover's pinch, which hurts, and is desired') should have such a bad press in these supposedly liberated times. What version of normality are we supposed to be swallowing? Who are the censors against whose authority masochism needs to be defended? What kind of mentality has produced its negative image?

I think there is a growing space for the more positive interpretation of masochism that I put forward here, an interpretation that comes from the side of art rather than science. I believe it could only come from art, that masochism can never be seen from a scientific perspective, though the scientist of integrity (Freud, for example) cannot help but see that there is something he or she is missing.

While researching and writing this book, I met few people who were left indifferent by the subject matter. Most people were ready, at a push, to confess to a little personal masochism. My dentist, whom I suspected to be inclined towards sadism, told me that she thought these things were 'the spice of life'. A close friend was fascinated by the idea that her sacrificial extremism about love, work and art could be considered not self-destructive but masochistically assertive. Discussing this released a tension in some people's minds, a tension between what they kept on doing and what they thought they ought to be doing. The conversation focused on a part of themselves that nobody had enabled them to describe, that remained outside, a threat and annoyance to self-worth.

Yes, there were also raised eyebrows, surprised laughs, demands for plenty of pictures to be included. An affable, shambling American poet recoiled nervously, saying it was 'a dangerous thing that people were scared of thinking about'. But there were few really starchy responses. At least among the kind of people I tend to meet, it seems that masochism is no longer considered a disgusting and unnatural tendency or something that ought to be weeded out of one's character through the raising of consciousness. For those who are open minded, perhaps masochism needs not defending, but explaining.

Yet there are many people who need to hear more of an argument. For these people, masochism is irrevocably linked to sleaze. 'Sleaze' is a new name for a fairly time-honoured set of institutions, exemplified in Britain by Conservative MPs lurking Priapus-like behind bushes or in brothels in seedy parts of South London, or prominent members of the criminal justice system being found kerb-crawling. These things have nothing to do with masochism or any other perversion, and everything to do with sexual and moral hypocrisy. Masochism may be dirty, but it isn't sleazy.

The confusion between the two arises from the common desire to remain respectable while also being pandered to and aroused in a quasi-sexual way, to be given a thrill at such a vicarious level that your conscience is not aroused. The popular newspapers cater shamelessly for this desire. As a child of about ten, I remember visiting a great-aunt who took one of these newspapers, and reading it with a mixture of horror and fascination – every other story was about rape or sexual murder. Only as an adult does one realize that such titillating subject matter is given a faint gloss of journalistic objectivity in order to spare the reader from becoming conscious of their own excitement.

Sexuality is only sleazy when it is sly and sneaky, when it pretends not to be there while surreptitiously seeking out its ends – the groper in the tube who has disappeared by the time you turn round, to find yourself surrounded by bland faces with innocuous expressions. Sleaze has a lot to do with the exclusion of a sexual aspect to one's normal persona. Sexual adventure is a different matter altogether. It results from being prepared to invent a life for yourself that is really worth living – rather than conforming to prevailing orthodoxies to the point where you become insensate, and need such vicarious, generally inadmissible thrills to get through the day.

Monogamy has to be made more fun than this. Sexual adventure can happen in couples, not just in special kinds of subcultures and groups who 'swing'. The creation of new forms of deviancy from the varieties of sexual experience has done few people any favours. Travelling the straight and narrow path of sexual 'normality' is likely to do nothing whatever for the essential feeling of being thoroughly, vibrantly alive, a feeling that everybody has had at some point in life but that for some is a distant memory. Continually repeating the same 'normal' position may not damage your health but it does get a little drab.

In the last couple of decades people have progressed a long way when it comes to thinking about sex. There are reference books and videos that tell you how to get the most out of it and assure you that sex is good for your health and well-being, rather like brown rice with alfalfa sprouts. It is something that we are encouraged to have in regular, moderated doses. But Woody Allen has a line about sex being no good unless it is dirty. Those who are into S/M would agree with him. At the same time as the proliferation of information about sexual manners and mores, there is a flourishing subcultural world which flaunts its sexual transgressiveness in the forms of sado-masochism, bondage and fetishism.

Sado-masochism as a stylistic subculture is a major influence and has been ever since Lou Reed and the Rolling Stones took over from the kind of clean-living pop groups that went before, and being charismatically bad became more popular than being dutifully good. That was a long time ago, but fashion continually revisits the sado-masochist's dressing-up box, refining and remodelling shiny plastic and skintight rubber into confrontational clothing. S/M is part of the image bank, no longer quite the shock to bourgeois good taste it once was, but offering a frisson of something dark and depraved.

Fashion, however – women's, at least – is a ground of competing influences, and at the opposite end of the spectrum from shiny leather and stilettos is the return of loose floral prints and long hair crimped into innocence. What the changeability of fashion indicates is that we never want to throw out an image of ourselves that we could possibly return to. Ideology – the desire to present oneself in a particular way – is also at war with this experimentalism, the sense of other selves, suppressed or potential, that want to become visible. Overtly feminine clothes make one conduct a different kind of relationship with the other person, suggesting a demure, narcissistic sensuality rather than a direct, challenging eroticism.

Sado-masochism as a fashion influence is a kind of stylistic expression of the war between the sexes, a war of power and seduction. But as a description of what two people do in bed (or on the floor, or against the wall), it is a misnomer. There is sadism, and there is masochism, and the two do not get on well together. The Marquis de Sade and Leopold von Sacher-Masoch, though both aristocrats, were divided not only by a century, but also by widely differing sexual perspectives. The sadist and the masochist are an impossible couple.

If the two were to get together, it would probably be due to some mutual misunderstanding and misinterpretation. The choice would be unusual – each partner might recognize that the other was not their usual type – and perhaps that in itself might be a motivation.

The sadist has to know that he is on top in a literal way, while the masochist is more sophisticated, a manipulator. Both want to direct the show, the first by force, the second by persuasion. Once, in the house where I used to live, we had a New Year's Eve party to which a group of guests brought along their friend, a tall, dark, saturnine intellectual, with the kind of Heathcliff looks that I do not usually respond to but this time did. We drank plenty of champagne and in classic style, got off together. But the ensuing sexual encounter proved unsatisfactory for both of us: he became loutish, I histrionic, and January the first was a day of hangovers rather than passion.

The two species are anything but complementary to each other; they are playing entirely different games. Sadism is characterized by a sullen, resentful apathy punctuated by bursts of self-pitying rage, in Sade's case directed at God and his mother-in-law. My sense of Sade's driving impulse is of violence fantasized as compensation for the feeling of being weighed down by an oppressive figure. It is as if the sense of being a creator were always collapsing into that of being a pawn in someone else's game, so an imaginative murder is needed, one that constitutes the creative act in itself and needs to be endlessly repeated and permuted. Sadism is a story of great pathos and even failure, in that the violence never accomplishes its goal of clearing a free space for action, for intervention into history.

Highly autonomous, the masochist's faults are vanity and posturing. While the sadist seeks a victim, and is repelled by the masochist's capacity for pleasure, which diminishes his own, the masochist wants to find a playmate. The opposite number is someone who can be convinced or charmed into acting the role of torturer, not a brutal heavyweight: that is why, as one frustrated masochist is quoted as remarking, 'a good sadist is hard to find'. No sadist is any good for a masochist, since each is disqualified from dancing to the other's tune, with the result that both are wrong-footed. The perfect choice may be another masochist.

The kind of sex we usually call sado-masochism is voluntary, consensual and, therefore, directed by masochistic rather than sadistic interests. Sadistic impulses are not collaborative ones, but rather test their effectiveness against the will of another person. Masochism needs collusion, because of the risk involved in submission. It cannot come into being without some form of relationship, a contractual bond or a mutual understanding, however ephemeral.

Sadism goes straight to its point: pleasure is to be had in violence against or domination of another person. Hollywood films have such a long tradition of responding to the demand for sadistic pleasure that they do it with sophisticated humour, for example in Quentin Tarantino's film *Pulp Fiction*.

Masochists are not a complementary breed to sadists, it is just that the binary dualism is so bright and shiny, so attractively user-friendly, that it has been convenient to go along with the idea that they are. Masochism is about a different kind of logic, an atmosphere of dangerous seduction, a deepening capacity for fascination. You might seek out somebody to embody all the things that seem bigger than you, that seem worth worshipping. You might have a wish to sense, from time to time, how small and insignificant you are. One Jungian analyst cites the case history of a woman who, increasingly successful in her career, feels a growing need for subjection, bondage and ritual humiliation. And it isn't just a cliché that formidable public figures seek private chastisement, sometimes at the hands of prostitutes: they have simply had enough of being on top.

A tired joke has it that the only way to hurt a masochist is to refuse to hurt him. This is true in that it would mean refusing to engage imaginatively in partnership with the masochist, refusing to enter their world. But it is not just a simple question of hurting. It is about being hurt in exactly the right way and at the right time, within a sophisticated, highly artificial scenario.

In common with most other people, those who are into masochism do not want to be hurt by the penal system. In the 1991 'Spanner' case, five men involved in consensual sado-masochistic sex were incarcerated under the Offences Against the Person Act. Despite its discreetness, this case shows that masochistic sex can still lead to prosecution or public victim-ization.

It would only seem odd for a woman to defend masochism if it were thought that women sexually enjoyed male violence or male bullying, and responded to it masochistically. Every-thing I know, including my own experience, indicates that we do not. Being a masochist and being a victim are different, even opposed. The victim has been forced on to the receiving end against her will, while the masochist has initiated a highly controlled situation involving bondage and pseudo-domination. Sometimes feminists use the term 'masochist' as a denigratory shorthand to mean 'the kind of woman who colludes with patriarchy'. But female subservience is not attributable to masochism, and these women may be responding to the generalized violence that male domination involves, seeming to collude while actually feeling forced.

The main problem for both sexes is in not enjoying one's masochism, because without enjoyment one is left uptight and self-pitying. In order to enjoy it, though, one has to learn to take control of it, to move into excitement with a sense of self-possession, to know one's boundaries and be ready to create something with a lover. The exploration of women's specific sexual capacities, longings and fascinations is something that *could* be put on to a feminist agenda, and in fact this is beginning to happen, with explorations of female fetishism and the growth of women's erotica. Men's unacknowledged masochism remains a dark continent. The recognition and assumption of masochism by both sexes could make for a more stimulating and enjoyable dynamic, a more pleasurable working out of power struggles, a dispersal of paranoia.

The way this book is written is highly subjective. It is not the articulation of some pre-existing system of thought, though I have certainly brought in insights from important thinkers on the subject. Finally, what concerns me most is lived experience, of which thought is only one component. Experience is, among other things, messy, dirty, painful, ambivalent, difficult to grasp, confusing, unpredictable, pathetic. Masochism is no tale of heroism; to understand it means being prepared to get into the disgusting and disgraceful side of yourself. Woody Allen's quip was a serious point for French novelist Jean Genet, who thought that to make art, it was important to get down into the dirt. That is what masochists always do, and what I am doing here.

1 Art into Sickness

The Case of the Missing Novelist

Leopold von Sacher-Masoch was born in Galicia, which is now part of Poland, in 1836, the son of a chief of police and an aristocratic mother. He proved brilliant at school, went on to study law but switched to history, and by the age of twenty was already lecturing at the University of Graz, Austria. Disappointed by the reception of his first book, an academic work, he decided to write fiction instead. He became a well-known and acclaimed writer whose works were swiftly translated into French and who was awarded a prestigious literary prize in Paris.

While editor of a literary journal, he began an affair with Fanny Pistor, author of short stories, drawing up a pseudo-legal contract by which he became her slave for six months in exchange for her wearing of furs. The two writers travelled to Italy together, with Leopold taking the name of Gregor and acting as Fanny's servant. The affair seems to have expired at the same time as the contract, but it inspired Sacher-Masoch's most famous novel *Venus im Pelz* (*Venus in Furs*), published in 1870.

Two years after the novel came out, Dr Richard von Krafft-Ebing arrived to take up the new chair of psychiatry and neurology at the University of Graz. Sacher-Masoch had given up teaching there, and the two men were never to meet, but it is more than likely that the psychiatrist heard frequent rumours about the writer through his links with the local bourgeoisie. The novelist's marriage, a year after Krafft-Ebing's arrival, to another aspirant writer who had taken the name Wanda after the fictional heroine of *Venus in Furs*, followed the pattern initiated by the affair with Fanny Pistor.

The psychiatrist worked in Graz for seventeen years and then left for the University of Vienna, from where he published a book on sexual psychopathology, giving the name of 'masochism' to a newly discovered perversion in men. He linked it to the existing tendency of sadism and described it as feminine and driven by morbid wishes. Sacher-Masoch's name had been truncated, reduced to lower case, the complexity and risk of his erotic explorations reduced to a single, generalized quantity. As Bernard Michel, his French biographer, remarks, this naming made a banality of Sacher-Masoch across every language, and killed him as a writer.

Sacher-Masoch rejected Krafft-Ebing's reconstruction of his name, but never went into print. If he thought it was a storm in a teacup, history quickly proved him wrong. Krafft-Ebing's books, including the encyclopaedia of the perversions, *Psychopathia Sexualis,* in which his researches on masochism were included, were a huge popular success. The perversities described in the book mirror the themes evoked in the decadent literature of that *fin-de-siècle* time – Huysmans, Wilde, Baudelaire – indeed they go much further. But the exploration is depersonalized, which is an essential difference between the creative literature of that time and this early sexology book. The sexual encyclopaedia, in its guise of satisfying an earnest quest for knowledge, speaks a desexualized language, and enacts a pseudo-repression under whose protection it deals with a wildly exotic range of subject matter, in the manner of anti-pornography campaigners who have to spend their whole time reading the most depraved material. The fundamental argument here is quite simple: 'It's not me, it's they who are the perverts,' or 'I'm just doing my job.'

In offering up masochism to general currency, the discourse of sexology irrevocably altered the public perception of

Sacher-Masoch's *oeuvre*. But is there anything worth salvaging? I would say that there are at least two aspects of his production that should be recognized and celebrated: that of the lived fiction, and second, but not in contradiction, the specific reworking of literary tradition.

There is certainly something of that quality of the classic that Ezra Pound calls 'irrepressible freshness' in the novels of Sacher-Masoch, perhaps because he tended to live his work and write of his life. The boundaries did not just overflow into each other: they positively energized and fuelled one another in a mutual dynamic which was playful, serious, extraordinarily productive and possibly rather exhausting. Thus Fanny Pistor, a budding author, contacts a Sacher-Masoch she knows from having read and admired his work: their affair follows fictional lines drawn up between them, to the extent of their taking on the names of quasi-fictional characters, acting out a fictional relationship between mistress and servant, and giving it the exciting foreign backdrop of Italy. A third, male character is sought after as an essential element, the rival, since betrayal is to be crucial to this *risqué* narrative.

While Sacher-Masoch's life is lived as literature because he plans it like that, his literature takes from life. *Venus in Furs* is the fictionalized account of Fanny and Leopold's real-life affair. It is worth remembering that his wife Wanda (who changed her real name, Aurora, to that of the novel's heroine) was also a writer of stories – indeed, she used her literary talents after her ex-husband's death to exploit his name and reputation ruthlessly. All this to make what ought to be an obvious point: Sacher-Masoch, at every level, is about fiction, and the lived life is a sophisticated, daring manipulation of reality. And masochistic experience, too, is a lived fiction, not sexological case history: any reading of it as such misses its fictive core, is a misreading or literalization. The masochist is a conscious manipulator, not a victim.

Venus in Furs is a demonstration of this. However much the hero Severin professes his amateurishness and his terror of Wanda, however much he stutters, demurs, or is paralysed, he will single-mindedly pursue his own pleasure and will systematically mould her to the dominatrix figure he needs to fulfil his desire. Much of the novel is taken up by the dialogue between the lovers, and during these conversations, Severin continually reiterates his desire for cruel treatment at the hands of a woman, Wanda in particular. 'It is because we are opposites – indeed almost enemies – that my love for you is part hatred, part fear. But in such relations, one person must be the hammer, the other, the anvil: I cannot be happy if I must look down on the woman I love. I want to be able to worship a woman, and I can only do so if she is cruel to me.' In this and many other such speeches, Severin puts forward a vision of love which gradually intoxicates Wanda.

What follows is a process of masochistic seduction, whose stages are as follows. Severin relates to her the stories of his previous love affairs – including the seduction of a mink-clad aunt who had beaten him as a child – and Wanda begins to be affected. She tells him that he has aroused her imagination, that he is 'the sort of man who will utterly corrupt a woman'. Wearing sable, she enters his room in the middle of the night, upon which Severin treats her to a learned discourse on the ecstatic cruelties of martyrdom, finally falling at her feet to propose a contract of slavery. The next day she asks him never to speak of such matters to her again, warning him twice of the dangers of his proposals. Soon after, she capitulates, and is drawn further and further into the role of torturess, yet at each stage begging to be released.

Wanda, the dominatrix, trails death behind her in the form of numerous rodents skinned for their fur, and of one swiftly mourned husband. This beautiful, wealthy widow is to make the perfect torturess for studious, stammering Severin: yet the roles of hunter and prey are oddly hard to allocate. And if there's a sadist in the picture, it certainly isn't Wanda.

If we were to rethink masochism along the lines laid down by Sacher-Masoch rather than Krafft-Ebing and his followers, we would be thinking of a kind of consciously planned risk-taking involving the education (or persuasion or corruption) of another person who would probably also be masochistic. Masochists implant ideas and fire the imaginations of others to draw them into their own visions of eroticism, so there is a strong capacity to formulate and plot and characterize – elements essential to the writing of novels.

Although his life makes gripping reading, and his imaginative facility must have helped him realize his masochistic desires, Leopold von Sacher-Masoch was not the originator of the theme of the cruel woman: it was a commonplace of romanticism and in particular of the decadent literature of the time. Literary historian Mario Praz showed that infatuation for the domineering woman who inspires a deadly fascination was a central theme in writings by numerous authors of the time, from Swinburne to Baudelaire, Huysmans to D'Annunzio. It is a theme that is particularly popular in the French tradition, which may account for the lionizing of Sacher-Masoch in Paris and for the more sympathetic treatment he has had in recent years from thinkers like Gilles Deleuze. Sacher-Masoch, destroyed by Vienna, has become readable again from within the French literary context in which he was, during his own lifetime, perhaps best understood.

How conscious was his antagonist, Dr Richard von Krafft-Ebing, of the widespread and deep-rooted literary traditions on which the Austrian novelist drew in his descriptions of supersensuality? Was he sensitive to the fact that what he was naming masochism was shared cultural currency? German romanticism seems to have kept itself relatively clear of sexual, decadent themes, in contrast to Italy, England and

France. Krafft-Ebing would have had to be a reader of contemporary foreign-language fiction to understand where Sacher-Masoch was coming from. But even if he recognized the connections, he was not ready to engage with these writers on anything but his own stubbornly simplified terms.

For Krafft-Ebing, Sacher-Masoch is a man afflicted by a sexual anomaly, both in his life and in his work. 'As an author he suffered severe injury as far as his work is concerned, for so long as and whenever he eliminated his perversion from his literary efforts, he was a gifted writer, and as such would have achieved real greatness had he been actuated by normally sexual feelings.' The psychiatrist here puts himself in the position of judging the relative merit of a poet's *oeuvre*. Could the novelist have been greater were he to have repressed his sexual tendencies? His most celebrated work is *Venus in Furs*, which explicitly treats of his sexual slavery to a woman.

The argument is wishful thinking. Would Sade's work have been rather more interesting were he less infatuated with cruelty, or Genet's greater with the criminality and homosexuality cut out? The sexual obsessions and particularities of writers, literary history shows, have been a storehouse of energy, inexhaustibly fuelling the production and shaping the nature of the emergent literary work. The difficulties and obsessions of the writer are the grit in the oyster that ultimately results in the pearl. And in any case a version of this argument could be, and was, turned on Krafft-Ebing himself.

The subject matter of his books covered mutilation of corpses, beast fetishism, defilement of statues, satyriasis and many other rare sexual tendencies, many now consigned to the dustbin of history. Nor were his works received with scientific disinterestedness by the readers of the time. A colleague of the psychiatrist remarked that the appearance of seven editions of *Psychopathia Sexualis* in six years could only be attributed to a pornographic interest on the part of the public. The *British*

Medical Journal of 1893 questioned whether his work should have been translated into English at all. To the psychiatrist's claim that he had chosen a title 'understood only by the learned' and that it seemed necessary also 'to give certain particularly revolting portions in Latin rather than German', the *BMJ* responded, 'Better if it had been written entirely in Latin, and thus veiled in the decent obscurity of a dead language.'

Krafft-Ebing plunders literature for his subject matter and then holds up the poet as a pathological object. It is not just Sacher-Masoch who gets this treatment: Baudelaire and the philosopher Rousseau also become case histories.

But these writers and thinkers were not patients who visited the psychiatrist to ask for help. Those who did became the curiously faceless objects of Krafft-Ebing's classifications, known only by occupation, sexual proclivity and odd physiological details. Baudelaire and Rousseau were the producers of seminal works of poetry or philosophy, which reveal an extensive and nuanced awareness of the more surprising, paradoxical and relatively unexplored areas of human behaviour. They knew they were complicated, and took a narcissistic and knowing pleasure in their own vicissitudes. Krafft-Ebing's representation of them as case histories followed a similar pattern to his treatment of Sacher-Masoch, where a rhetorically sophisticated, poetically charged literary language is reduced and displaced to a dry, simple, normative account.

Freud was to become a junior colleague of Krafft-Ebing's at the University of Vienna and received encouragement from the older man. When he came to work on the question of masochism, he brought to it a vastly greater intellect and powers of speculation and analysis. Yet he did not challenge some of Krafft-Ebing's fundamental tenets, neither the link to morbid desires postulated by the psychiatrist, nor the idea of a complementarity with sadism.

Meanwhile the novels of Leopold von Sacher-Masoch had

gradually been abandoned by the reading public. His story of Severin, the sensitive intellectual who engineers his own afflictions as an unorthodox manner of achieving manhood, had become unreadable except as soft porn. The particularities of his fictional world – the glamorous milieux in which elegant small-talk conceals terrorist intentions, the protagonists' sexual and emotional vertigo, his manner of dealing with political issues – had all become invisible.

Masochism, the offspring of art abducted and operated on by science, an odd hybrid creature, surgically patched together from disparate parts like Frankenstein's monster, had begun its journey into the theoretical apparatus of twentieth-century psychoanalysis.

The Contract

A couple makes a contract in which he agrees to become her slave for that day. Both of them must abide by certain rules, violation of which automatically invalidates the deal. They invent fictional, exotic names for each other to be used solely for the duration of the contract, names which emphasize her role as dominatrix and his as slave. She agrees to wear a particular pair of high-heeled shoes. They write down the details and sign their assumed names to the contract. During that day, his will is totally suspended, he responds only to hers and can be physically punished for any supposed shortcomings. For her there is the luxurious feeling of command and a certain enjoyment of complete possession of her object, knowing that his desire must remain repressed. When they make love, it is in the manner she chooses, and she may choose to satisfy herself and not him.

Both of them work hard to inhabit their roles fully, since they are normally an egalitarian couple who negotiate matters.

For that reason alone, these changed circumstances are exhilarating, allowing them to occupy the less reconstructed parts of themselves that linger on from childhood, or the fantasy parts of themselves made up from a collage of heroes and villains from novels and the cinema. The changed style of interacting requires a continual imaginative commitment – it is not easy to achieve – but both of them enjoy ranging over the new terrain that they have mapped out together. It is a private game, a psychosexual adventure, primitive and sophisticated at once, relying on trust, humour, acting ability and emotional elasticity.

This is one possible masochistic scenario, fairly closely modelled on the classic contract of Severin and Wanda in Sacher-Masoch's novel. This is the kind of thing we are dealing with, though masochism has become a kind of catch-all category into which all sorts of disparate elements have been cast.

Dictionary definitions of masochism will tell you that it is a perversion consisting of the enjoyment of your own humiliation or pain. But what other elements emerge as essential to the scenario described above? First of all, agreement between the two members of the couple: a short-term contract. Second, the fictional or fantasy element, changed names, exotic role-playing. Third, adventure, exploration of other selves, a sophisticated, daring playfulness. And fourth, effort – the two people are interested enough in their relationship not just to launch the contract but to sustain it to the end (how many couples could actually be bothered, after the washing up is done?)

We could make an interim definition of masochism as follows, then. It is the agreement between two people to explore the roles of master and slave by acting them out for a specified time period. Across the pages of this book, I hope to enrich and make complex that basic picture, perhaps even to change it altogether, but this will do as a starting point.

In contrast to the subjective fluidity of the two people here, their capacity to construct and act out a kind of play that enables them to move in and out of the neglected or unexplored aspects of themselves, is the rather self-conscious theory that has attempted to analyse masochistic phenomena.

Early psychiatry named masochism, and this naming came about in a particularly unsympathetic, even violent way. But psychoanalysis inherited the concept, kept it alive, and tried to make it perform a minor role in the Freudian opera. When we use the term 'masochism', we cannot help but be complicit with this tradition, in the same way that the term 'inversion' (meaning homosexuality) has negative connotations due to its historical currency as a perversion in normative psychoanalysis.

All of this sounds unpromising. Having said that, psychoanalysis is where we have to go to find out more about masochism, it is the place where we expect to locate that thinking. Freud's stature has made him an essential reference point for the thinkers of this century, who have appreciated in him, among other things, the integrity of the scientist who returns to a point of difficulty. Masochism challenged Freudian thought in a particular way, stimulated some of its most perceptive passages. It is Freud's work that has enabled a debate on masochism to emerge, primarily through two sympathetic commentators, Leo Bersani and the late Gilles Deleuze, over the last two or three decades.

The debate has also opened up outside psychoanalysis. One reason for this may be illustrated by a comment of Adam Phillips (no relation) in his book *On Flirtation*, when he says that psychoanalysis 'unavoidably promotes and institutionalizes the idea of the exemplary life'. It may be that masochism simply cannot be absorbed into the psychoanalytic view of a good way to live: it has not been so far, at any rate.

Freud did discover important things about masochism, but those discoveries tend to be surrounded by a quite personal and tangible sense of unease with the question, and they are insights that are not easily placed or fully interpreted.

His 1924 essay 'The Economic Problem of Masochism' was the single time that he explicitly addressed the question, though he certainly touches on it elsewhere. Looking briefly at this piece should be useful. First, as a reminder of what kinds of conceptual ingredients went into the making of our contemporary view, and second, as an indicator of the background web of associations, the dangerous atmosphere with which masochism seems surrounded, for the psychoanalyst.

The essay begins by describing masochism as an enigma, a mysterious, inexplicable human tendency that does no good to the human organism. The psychoanalyst cannot find masochism's usefulness, beginning as he does with the premise that each organism is oriented fundamentally towards its own benefit and advancement. Searching for a functional role for masochism, Freud is stumped. Following the essay is like accompanying a blind man in a maze. The expedition is one of short, nervous ambles forward followed by sudden halts and then abrupt alterations of direction.

Not only, continues Freud, is there no economic function for masochism, it is also actually threatening, extremely dangerous for the organism. He has neglected the fact that sexual pleasure is central to the masochistic encounter and seems to see nothing but a person who accepts pain or humiliation. Masochism, he asserts, paralyses the pleasure principle, the agency that has a protective and benevolent influence over mental life. What Freud seems to be seeing in the masochist – like many others since his time – is the willing victim, the person who docilely accepts punishment rather than standing up for himself. If masochism were really like that, then this book would not be defending it. (I can think of a number of reasons why someone would adopt that position, from fatalism to pragmatism, but none of them involve the erotic, perverse and self-determining elements that are an essential part of masochistic make-up.)

27

Dragging sadism into the picture again, Freud says that masochism is, by comparison, far more of a threat – even if masochistic tortures rarely take the extreme forms that sadistic cruelties do – because the sadist gets rid of his or her deadly tensions on to an outside world, while the masochist, in his view, pushes his own inside and accepts more from elsewhere. This is a radically antisocial position: the analyst is concerned only with the patient in the consulting room, not with the network of people with whom he does and will come into contact. There is an inbuilt potential here for the patient, the analysand, to develop a will to power which takes him beyond the promptings of common humanity. What helps and heals one person, according to this view, can perhaps only be obtained at the expense of others' well-being. The instinct towards pleasure, however cruelly it is obtained, Freud thinks, protects the psyche, while the desire for pain or humiliation threatens and damages the one who desires. Freud's view of an exemplary life was perhaps a tougher one than today's psychoanalytic community would be ready to promote.

The attractiveness of this argument rests on its reversal of common-sense views – usually one thinks of the murderer, the violent aggressor, as being mentally ill, but within the Freudian schema he or she may be a thriving individual who repudiates the sickly promptings of conscience, and in particular the Christian conscience. Someone rather like Nietzsche's idea of the strong, untrammelled pagan, driven by an appetite to expend himself, to kill. But the image of the joyful killer is oddly unconvincing, and few would imagine the human rights violator, the sex murderer, in this way. Freud's polemical position is a defence of individual egoism against the pressure of social mores. Where Sacher-Masoch's protagonist Severin wanted to be the anvil, Freud wants to be on the side of the hammer. To the credit of both authors, they end in failure, being carried forward by their own logic towards another place.

Back to the essay. Freud begins the task of interpreting the phenomenon of masochism, finding a place for it. Noting that many masochistic fantasies consist of 'being gagged, bound, painfully beaten, whipped, in some way maltreated, forced into unconditional obedience, dirtied and debased', he draws the conclusion that the masochist wishes to be treated as a small and helpless child, a naughty child. He is suggesting that the desire is for a return to an event in infancy, a real event, a regression to an infantile state.

There is an obvious objection to this proposal. Parents do not, in general, bind and gag, whip or painfully beat, dirty or debase their children, in response to acts of naughtiness – and never did. Such fantasies do not remind us of events in infancy, except perhaps of moments when we were being bullied by other children. And that would be quite different, because there would be no question of crime, punishment, parental authority; just the amoral flow of impulses between peers or siblings.

There are other objections: why must we immediately refer back to childhood? Is not sexual fantasy often about things of which we have little or no knowledge, about things that happen to other people, frequently about things that we very much *do not* want to happen to us in real life? It seems to me that erotic fantasy is rarely set in the past, rarely rakes up old events, and almost never childhood ones. Certain materials (mud, fur, even certain kinds of food) may have a strong sensual and psychological meaning due to moments in childhood or adolescence that had an aura of sensuality around them – but there is nothing regressive in this kind of sensual nostalgia. Erotic fantasy is never literal enough to relive any event, it takes place in a bric-a-brac world lived out in tension with the present. It involves the sense of a safe enclosure and the manipulation of exciting motifs to stimulate and articulate sexual pleasure. That feeling of safety may be why many

29

women admit to enjoying rape fantasies, and though this may be slightly embarrassing and hard to reconcile with feminist perspectives, few of us genuinely worry about it, because it tends not to be acted out and remains a pleasantly erotic diversion.

Freud is straining credulity by invoking childhood as a place to which all signposts point, even in fantasy. Do we really believe we have been here before? Masochistic scenarios are characterized by the setting-up of master-slave relationships, not parent-child ones. The iconography of bondage, rubber, whips and chains is a far cry from the symbols and images of infancy. (In Japan there is a sexual service industry in babying adult men, bottle-feeding them and so on: this nostalgia for maternal soothing contrasts strongly, however, with the dark, tough edginess of the sado-masochistic encounter.)

If we go a little further with Freud, having encountered masochism as both dangerous and mysterious on one hand, yet on the other, transparently childish, a further characterization seems to arise almost inevitably, to resolve the contradictions with apparent ease. Masochism is feminine, Freud says, it places the subject in a female situation. (The whole essay is only concerned with male masochism, in the tradition of Krafft-Ebing.)

Freud pastes femininity on to masochism, as if the former in itself could be made accountable for masochism's status as a perversion. After being asked to see masochism as infantile, we are now to be convinced that it is feminine. Of course a male masochist may take up the position of a submissive woman. But this is by no means a central or defining quality – for example, there is no transvestism or other kind of feminization of the male protagonists of Sacher-Masoch's novels. A man does remain a man even after erotic humiliation, and men involved in masochism may symbolically endanger their masculinity in order to test and fulfil themselves as men. This is not a side issue; it is the key aim to a certain kind of masochistic exposure.

Freud continues to wrestle with the pathology. The third proposition is hard to reconcile with the previous ideas of a regression to infancy or of a male transsexual: now we are faced with a guilt-ridden person obsessed with the idea of having committed a crime, and who seeks out torment and punishment. Not a bad idea, but why make it pleasurable, in that case? Why wouldn't someone like this rather join a puritan religious sect, for example, and have to endure all kinds of deprivations without the erotic solaces of masochism?

Freud admits, almost immediately after, that 'this looks like a superficial rationalization of the masochistic subject matter'. But that does not indicate that any more interesting developments are on their way. Rather he goes back to first base, proposing a link to infantile masturbation, which remains undeveloped. As it well might.

This kind of language is not going anywhere near the body it discusses. Of course, language never succeeds in the incarnation of experience, but perhaps it is at its worst when attempting to describe pain. Descriptions of pain can at best produce a wince, a tremor of horror – but how indescribably worse is the actual experience. People can share most things, but physical pain is an exception. In fact, when someone you love is in pain it is particularly sad, because you feel removed from that person: no one can feel another's pain. If pain is inextricably linked to pleasure, an existential isolation appears, perhaps at the heart of the couple, where warmth and sharing is usually expected. This double solitude can be understood as another aspect of how things are, a truthfulness that can be lightly assumed. Speaking or discoursing upon this kind of experience is as hard as evoking the flavour of a pomegranate to someone who has never tasted its seeds.

For Freud, the truth is rarely lightly assumed. In this essay it becomes mythical and universal. In a more exalted mood, he moves away from the regressive, feminine, masturbatory interpretations of masochism to rediscover it as an expression of Thanatos, the death instinct. Having intended to promote the health-giving pursuit of pleasure, Freud seems forced to recognize deadly impulses as the most fundamental. Erotogenic masochism enters this much more ambitious picture as a tendency whose extensive power has for the first time been recognized. Like sadism, it is made up of a combination of death instinct and libido. But it is the part that cannot safely be exorcised through action in the world, that hangs on grimly to the organism whatever happens.

So masochism is not just something morbid, not just an expression of death drive, but a mixture of two opposing wishes, for life *and* for death, for the gratification of pleasure *and* the desire to engage with the downside – for example, the need to repeat unpleasant experiences. This gives a picture of masochism as universal, no longer a perversion but something that everybody has to handle (or be handled by) in one way or another.

Freud's insights here are important because they give a complex view of how human beings are, one that goes far beyond the notion of the cure. This perspective recognizes how ineradicable are human confusion, ambivalence and sickness, alongside health, clarity and sanity. And it is masochism that holds on to all of this at once, at the eye of the storm. Masochism that refuses to let the demons be exorcized, sent out into the world to wreak damage elsewhere, that stubbornly holds on to this impossible life-death cocktail, *somewhere inside*.

It is always there as a possibility. But how, in what circumstances and under which conditions, does the tendency become a physical and emotional reality? When does the excitement begin?

2 The Overspill

Pain and Pleasure Revisited

I have described Krafft-Ebing and Sacher-Masoch, the two aristocratic intellectuals living simultaneously in Graz, as antagonists. But there are similarities in their views, particularly in the way they relate to their readers, incorporating into their writings techniques that defuse the impact of the controversial material both of them presented.

Krafft-Ebing, as I have shown, claimed to present scientific material objectively while thoroughly indulging a general public in its desire for descriptions of bizarre sexual proclivities. What he had understood was the tactical necessity to protect readers from themselves, or rather from the conscious knowledge of their own participatory pleasure. Sacher-Masoch was doing the same kind of thing within a different discipline, using various literary devices to frame his narratives and make them somehow decent, circumventing at least superficially the reader's repressions. So, for example, in *Venus in Furs* he has the story told by one young man to another in the trustful intimacy of a cosy hearthside setting. And in this and other novels he creates misty, romanticized backdrops and wraps up his novels with sanitized endings – all sparing the reader from conscious identification with the material, instead of which he or she ranges over a terrain of vicarious, disavowed pleasure. Even Severin's name for his own preferred form of eroticism, 'supersensualism', has a chocolate-box lyricism.

Both novelist and psychiatrist offer perverse, rather than transgressive, ways of reading masochism; neither of them is ready to get his hands dirty by attempting consciously to apologize for pleasure. This is where Freud differs, befriending eroticism, showing how important stimulus is, how it boosts the appetite for life. And it was he who made the fundamental discovery that *everything that affects us intensely becomes sexual, including pain and displeasure.*

This observation seems counter-intuitive. We tend to assume that we want to avoid pain, and though few of us are brave enough to admit to the untrammelled cultivation of pleasure, we certainly recognize its immense attractions. If Freud is right, it would lead to a kind of practical self-doubt about how to conduct personal preferences, along what lines to organize ourselves, in fact how to interpret the varying flavours of existence, how to live. Given this perspective, you can begin to look again at a whole range of actions in more complex terms. A friend makes you feel intensely inferior, yet you keep on seeing him or her; the intensity of your own reaction is a form of stimulus. You love jazz, soul, and late seventies pop, yet insist on going with your lover to concerts of atonal modern music that leave you excited but defeated – it is not just intellectual pretension, but a longing for the sublime sense of exile of that super-rational absolutism. If lack of pleasure is strong enough it can become erotic, stimulating, exciting.

Giving equal roles in life to displeasure or suffering and to pleasure means that you can no longer dress up your addictions with high moral terminology. Heroism and self-sacrifice are no longer simply admirable, because every possible role involves some erotic satisfaction. (Freud asserts that even the act of committing suicide offers some level of pleasure to the individual.)

Explicitly sexual masochism is a recognition of this paradox, challenging the quiet eroticism and togetherness espoused by the kind of sexology that promotes norms, and showing how troubled, difficult encounters push through the body's responsiveness to extreme sexual pleasure. The positions of torturer and victim are assumed as forms of role playing, since sexual pleasure is the aim.

An instance of this takes place and is reported in an earthy, comic way a century before Freud by the eponymous heroine of John Cleland's *Fanny Hill*, an English libertine novel. Fanny, a young prostitute, entertains a client who lashes her bottom with a twig. She is not happy with this kind of treatment, but her good humour revives with a little shared supper. Then a surprising alteration of mood occurs.

> ... a change so incredible was wrought in me, such violent yet pleasingly irksome sensation took possession of me that I scarce knew how to contain myself: smart of the lashes was now converted into such a prickly heat, such fiery tinglings, as made me sigh, squeeze my thighs together, shift and wriggle about my seat with furious restlessness; whilst these itching ardours, thus excited in those parts on which the storm of discipline had principally fallen, detached legions of burning, subtile, stimulating spirits, to their opposite spot and centre of assemblage, where their titillation raged so furiously that I was even stinging-mad with them.

Fanny has discovered that painful feelings can spill over into sexual desire. And if pain can become pleasure through some strange alchemy, perhaps pleasure itself is not so easily understood as we thought. Pleasure turns against itself in the state of mind which a person experiences when feeling jaded – a paralysing, stuffy, weary, bored, self-disgusted, wilted feeling that appears after a surfeit of pleasure. This condition has not, to my knowledge, been analysed, perhaps because of its ambiguous nature. Pleasure has moved back into displeasure, has found a place where it is no longer singular, where it becomes a loathsome sensation of passivity, of your individuality being suffocated. What would be the cure? Think of the words: discipline, challenge, purification, ordeal, *suffering*. Paganism reaches its limits and longs for a breath of fresh air; the Romans who flocked to the arena to enjoy watching Christians being torn apart by lions and bears later became the most assiduous converts. The drive of appetite with an absolutely natural logic gives way to the longing for mortification. There is something in pleasure's satisfaction that is distinctly unpleasant.

This again seems to show that the conscience or superego has much in it that is desired. Unless suffering and discipline from an external source are part of one's life, as they are for many people who find themselves exploited due to race, class or sex, one *might* seek them out through a stronger relation to the ethical imperative. Oscar Wilde made the suggestion that the wealthy classes were, in general, 'more moral, more intellectual, more well behaved' than the poor. It was not long before he discovered his espousal of the upper classes to be distinctly misplaced. But one can see how it could be true, if freedom from want and suffering were understood for the opportunity it opens up – the opportunity to build the soul, and not necessarily in a morbid way.

Those greediest for pleasure, then, or those to whom pleasures come easily, tend to find they need the salutary corrective of suffering, which comes in many forms, one of them sexual sado-masochism. Masochism is one way of bringing together a Christian contempt of the flesh with a pagan delight in it, and *Venus in Furs* has Severin taking the first perspective and Wanda the second. Masochists are not weak, although they may decide to act out that role. Actually, strength and vitality are likely to be their primary traits – as in the mischievous, enterprising heroine of *Fanny Hill*.

It can be objected that there is another kind of masochist,

one more like the figure that Isabella Rossellini plays in David Lynch's film *Blue Velvet*, much darker and more depressive. Her masochism seems to emerge from the other end of the spectrum, in which desperate suffering is turned into a kind of triumph, when she demands that her younger lover, Kyle MacLachlan, hit her. She is repeating, on her own terms, a sexual violence that has been forced upon her by the psychotic Dennis Hopper. She also makes art from the situation as a night-club singer, and finally, she survives when both her husband and his murderer do not. Blue velvet turns out to be not just seductive to the touch but also a resilient material.

The least one can say, then, is that pain and pleasure are not always absolute opposites, or that if they are, they are opposite kinds of the same thing, intense stimulation. It seems that the term 'masochism' can be used as a kind of bag into which every mixed experience is thrown, every perception of extreme excitement that is neither purely enjoyable nor unremittingly nasty. But how often is any experience really so pure? And how many strange species must exist in this shady shelter – oddly inexpressible feelings, kinds of ambiguity, possibly shameful, possibly secretly smug – like the insect life on ground level of the all-American lawn in *Blue Velvet*, a subculture of intense violence, neglected but ever present, threatening the self-evident niceness of the clean-living culture above.

Contemporary literary theorist Leo Bersani suggests that sexual pleasure may be identical to a kind of pain, and points out how difficult it is to articulate such matters of corporeal feeling in language.

What about poetic language? There is a distinct temptation to see the literary tradition as holding most of the answers when it comes to masochism. Literature is an extremely ancient tradition which since at least Ovid's time has dealt implicitly with a kind of love we now describe as masochistic.

37

The thirteenth-century love allegory *The Romance of the Rose* is an interesting example. Guillaume de Lorris describes the moment when the lover falls in love with the rose in terms that evoke the fear and pain allied to extreme attraction:

> ... when I smelled its exhalation, I had no power to withdraw, but would have approached to take it if I had dared stretch out my hand to it. But the sharp and piercing thorns that grew from it kept me at a distance. Cutting, sharp spikes, nettles, and barbed thorns allowed me no way to advance, for I was afraid of hurting myself.

Over the centuries the comparison of love to a red rose has become so commonplace as to descend into a St Valentine's day cliché that only a novelist like Jean Genet could redeem, *The Miracle of the Rose* reinvesting it with its full passionate potential. But why would the rose ever have become such a compelling symbol of love if not for its cruelly piercing thorns? At any rate, the incapacity of language to describe the eroticism that Bersani highlights seems more applicable to psychoanalysis than it is to literature, which has been whispering, stammering, about the exquisite agonies of erotic love for millennia.

Must we use a literal language to describe intense sensations at all, when a sophisticated alternative, poetic literature, does it better? My provisional answer to this question would be yes, because public debate is informed by the essay rather than the novel or poem, and masochism is a live issue for contemporary culture, crossing issues of feminism, gay rights, redefinitions of masculinity, mental health and even of what kind of sex is legal. There is a need for an explicit address of these questions, if only because clearing the path of misconceptions can reveal new ways of thinking, acting, living. Literature is not best placed to service debate in a direct sense, though it is an invaluable reference source for it – its world is intimacy and subtle exploration, through the human voice.

Bersani's significant move, which involves bringing literature together with psychoanalytic readings, is to displace
masochism from its traditionally peripheral position as a sexual aberration and set it at the centre of the sexual stage. He
does this by developing Freud's description of primary erotogenic masochism, the kind that occurs whenever stimulus of
an unpleasant kind becomes strong enough to spill over into
sexual pleasure. Bersani does not concern himself with views
about what is either normal or pathological, but rather with
asking what the valid principles are that create sexual impulses.
So while for Freud the discovery of primary masochism still
at work during adulthood constitutes perversion, for Bersani it
is the core of the erotic. He goes on to create a closely argued
theory of how this overspill of sensation is crucial in the making of art and literature. Bersani's work gives a psychoanalytic
answer as to why literature has concerned itself for so long
with masochistic experience.

He coins a key term, 'self-shattering *jouissance*'. *Jouissance*
is a word that is difficult to translate exactly because of its
deployment in a specific theoretical history, but for our purposes here it means an extreme kind of joy that occurs when a
defined sense of self is ruptured. It can also quite simply mean
'orgasm': it belongs to that order of ecstatic experience, so the
term 'pleasure' is now being supplanted by a much more full-
blooded concept.

Any intense experience – sex, art, even fleeting, momentary
perceptions like the effect of inhaling the scent of a flower –
can lead to an overpowering, self-shattering emotion, and in
general we like the fact that we can be moved by such things.
But the feeling of intense arousal of any kind is also painful, a
surge of fluids that may result in tears, that demands immediate discharge. Becoming aroused in this way is a matter of conflict: it is a commonplace that women are more prone to
outbursts of emotion while men tend to erupt sexually, but

whether this is true or not there are times when the negative side of the equation dominates: you decide you cannot stand the loss of control, so the experience is avoided. Sometimes this dampening down of difficult feelings becomes almost total. Poet and anthropologist Michel Leiris remarks in his autobiography *Manhood* that despite being prone to weeping as a child and adolescent, as an adult he is completely incapable of tears, even if the only thing that he feels proud of in himself is a kind of fervour.

If a level of responsiveness reminds us that there is something in there to respond, that we aren't just deadpan workers and consumers, it is also a risky business. You don't necessarily calculate the odds, but everyone has their own individual sense of how much of this kind of risk they are prepared to engage in, how much to play safe. One gauge of this is cultural adventurousness, the appreciation of the challenge of new forms of art. In New York it's the democracy of the gallery scene, twelve openings in the same Broadway building on the same night, with greedy, wide-awake crowds surging from an exhibition of pop-art collages to a display next door of high-gloss documentary photographs. Paris must be the only capital that treats its *littérateurs* like pop stars or politicians, giving them the job of reinterpreting and commenting on historical events, making every kind of café talk fizz from their pronouncements on Aids, post-colonialism, and *la différence*. The engagement with new artistic forms is what enables metropolitan life to go beyond itself in an exciting contact which causes first a breakdown of identity, then an invigoration of it.

Risk-taking, embracing the unknown, requires confidence, and not all cultures or people are capable of it. But the shattering experience is ultimately rewarding: for example, the sense of healing, even of euphoria, that occurs after a flood of tears, or the sense of absolute relaxation after orgasm. Something has been discharged, almost in the sense that we discharge a debt, even with an analogous kind of relief. The alternative is to seal yourself off from external threat, to go for invulnerability. But while this protects you from the outside world, armour is heavy and noisy and does not allow a flow between interior and exterior, causing a kind of irritable stagnation and a loss of nerve.

So one of the things that a self-shattering *jouissance* has to offer, one of the important aspects of primary masochism, is that it allows a kind of refreshment or renewal. Fanny finds her adventure with her client 'ultimately much more to my satisfaction than I had bespoke the nature of it to turn out'. That is the reason why the game is worth playing.

The Tortured Artist

Are artists more masochistic than other people? Is that the fundamental sense of the myth of the tortured artist, the romantic figure, addicted to narcotics, sexual promiscuity, self-destruction? One might think of the painter Jean-Michel Basquiat, German film-maker Rainer Werner Fassbinder, or the actress Edie Sedgwick; all were phenomenally talented, all died young. Bankers and technocrats, accountants and lawyers, are not known to walk on the wild side. Artists do, and not just in the popular imagination.

Is it that composers, painters, sculptors are so infatuated with the overwhelming stimuli around them that they bypass any investment in psychological insurance policies? Is it that they either have a willingness to take the risks that lead to shattering and renewal, or simply are somehow more exposed to what is out there, as if they are burnt by the sun? Or could there be another factor involved, one that could account for qualities of shrewdness, the way that artists are creatively self-serving?

American video artist Bill Viola described, in a recent book, how our sensory faculties could be seen to limit the intake of energies or information from the outside world. This view, derived from the philosopher Henri Bergson, challenges the common-sense idea that they are there to take it all in. Viola's Bergsonian view is close to Bersani's idea that we need protection from overwhelming levels of external stimulus. But it specifically focuses on what the five senses do: by taking in some of what is around us, we exclude the enormity of the universe, which would, perhaps, destroy us. From this perspective the artist's perceptive faculties can be seen as faulty, unable to do properly their job of shutting off reality. What I have been describing as a mark of confidence and vitality can be viewed in another light as a malfunction that leaves particular people existentially vulnerable.

The freshness and power of an artistic production is dependent on the artist's extreme response to the world, although that response also has to be refiltered and represented through the demands of the discipline at a particular moment. This makes it sound simple, but the difficulty is that the two processes of engagement with the world and engagement with the medium are in a kind of dynamic struggle. The stimulus caused by the original experience is sublimated, that is, put to work on behalf of the highest impulses, rather than just enjoyed. Yet the enjoyment is not to be lost in the process, because it is this level of excitement that energizes the whole activity. This theory of creativity would apply to cool modernism or to eclectic post-modernism as well as to more obviously expressive forms of art such as romanticism. But how does such sublimation occur? There is an argument that can be described as developmental. It is about how tiny infants learn to cope with the enormity of the world around them.

The psychic mechanisms that are instrumental begin early. French psychoanalyst Jean Laplanche proposes that the infant has to arrive at a moment when he or she begins to introject objects from the outside world. This is the beginning of the capacity to fantasize – and it is the first moment of psychological suffering that the infant undergoes. At the same time, whether or not the content of the fantasy is agreeable, it is highly exciting – in a sense that is both auto-erotic and masochistic. Laplanche argues that the very movement of fantasy, its constitution, in which something external is brought within one's own psyche, is masochistic. It is, therefore, a privileged and essential aspect of human sexuality.

This then becomes the pattern for sexuality in adult life. Sexual arousal happens when a stimulus is so perturbing, so intolerable, that one's sense of a controlling self breaks down. Masochism is the ground of sexuality, not an individual aberration: what we seek in it is a kind of ecstatic pain, a bodice-ripping, an overwhelming physical sensation.

For the small child, this introjection, this imagining of the suffering, devastated position is protective and beneficial. Though it may seem sad to us that even a tiny infant has the capacity for such melancholic feelings, in fact it is valuable for the infant, defending the psyche against the overwhelming arousal of the environment. At the point where the psychic organization breaks down from exposure to levels of stimuli greater than it can bind or neutralize, sexuality takes over.

It is a fundamental human capacity: the monster is there from the start. In Mary Shelley's novel *Frankenstein*, the narrator comes from the kind of family in which there is never a cross word. And from this kindly, liberal, gentle background erupts its antithesis, the massively strong creature with surging, uncontrollable drives, who loves with unbelievable tenacity and kills demonically when he finds himself unloved. The monster – the alien, or the Tyrannosaurus rex in Steven Spielberg's *Jurassic Park* – is charismatic, dispersing fear by making it visible.

43

(Violence itself tends to be lacklustre in comparison with its imaginative representations, managing to be both dreary and traumatic at the same time. The gore and splat of *Pulp Fiction* is fun to watch, but when you see the same blood-red colour spread on the side of a motorway, alongside ambulance workers settling prone figures into stretchers, the emotional reaction is quite different.)

The idea of artistic oversensitivity, of a too-keen perceptive level is only half of the story; it would only explain, in fact, some kinds of madness. And artists have a living to earn, to make themselves useful in a somewhat mean and sceptical world, a world that knows easier ways to get its kicks. They have to gain a particular knowledge, train themselves to become transformers. So the painter Whistler, when challenged for charging two hundred guineas for a painting of two days' work, replied that he asked it for the knowledge of a lifetime.

In order to work, artists have to be prepared to become erotically stimulated and charged, to open themselves to a high level of excitement at the very beginning. This may go some way to explaining the popularity of the female nude in painting, as a subject matter that could, in the heterosexual male, be stimulating enough to provoke the artistic process. Objects of extreme beauty, terror or pathos, anything that produces an intense response in the artist, sets off this process. Like the tiny child, the artist is overwhelmed by the stimulus to the point of a breakdown of psychological control: unlike the infant, he has put himself in this position deliberately.

Instead of releasing the intense response into direct sexuality, artists hold on to it and allow themselves to be driven by it. This is, of course, a description of the well-known phenomenon of sublimation. What I am pointing out is that there is always something painful about this level of excitement, and that artists are unusual both in their capacity to risk psychological rupture and in their ability to transform excitement into energy, energy into aesthetic achievement.

In other words, artists are nothing if not *professional* masochists, people who have intuitively grasped the fact that certain impulses can be treated so as to become a product in the real world, people who have understood how to work with those impulses, go with the flow, make something of them. Artists are productive masochists.

These claims run counter to the normative view of masochism, to find in it a central spring of sexual life and an imaginative fount. But there is, of course, a downside, and this book cannot become a straightforward apology for masochism.

The subject is not quite that tame, the capacity for a transformation of internal intensities into the magical is double edged, never fully controllable. The safe spillage that creativity allows may not always be transferable to other areas of life. I think of the American Indians who were employed to work on building the Manhattan skyscrapers, and who refused to use safety gear, no matter what the weather: this enabled them to deploy all their agility and heroism, but it also led occasionally to spectacular deaths.

3 Belladonna

Collusion Theory

How gender-specific is the discussion so far, how determined by masculine interests? What about the sexual politics of all this? Could women who behave masochistically merely be giving in to male domination (and if so, what would they be getting out of it)?

This is a very recent kind of question, one that would have made no sense a century ago. At that time, to be masochistic was virtually synonymous with being feminine. As we have seen, Krafft-Ebing and then Freud, both confining their remarks to a perversion in men, found it to be a feminine tendency: for the former, 'a morbid degeneration of mental qualities specifically feminine', for the latter, 'an expression of the feminine nature'.

Masochism comes to the attention of psychiatry as a problem when it appears in the male, while masochistic women are not yet counted as perverts. The notion of perversion itself is much debated, particularly by gay thinkers like Jonathan Dollimore, and I shall discuss this later, but for the present I will simply cite a definition taken from *The Language of Psychoanalysis* by Laplanche and Pontalis: 'deviation from the "normal" sexual act when this is defined as coitus with a person of the opposite sex directed towards the achievement of orgasm by means of genital penetration'.

The idea of perversion is dependent on the subscription to a norm, heterosexual genital sex. This kind of distinction – in which normality is at the centre and all the other kinds of sexuality thrown into a kind of mixed bag of horrors – is quite confusing, in that they are left each unexplored and considered equivalently abnormal. Thus masochism is one of the many tendencies coagulated together in this conception, alongside harmful non-consensual practices like paedophilia and bestiality. Masochism, according to the same dictionary, is defined as a 'sexual perversion in which satisfaction is tied to the suffering or humiliation undergone by the subject'.

As the authors point out, neither the sexologists nor Freud after them were intending such descriptions to apply to women. (Perhaps women did not complain of any problem.) What was sauce for the goose was definitely not sauce for the gander. Women were being considered as *essentially* masochistic, in a sense that required little comment. The element of transsexuality – men participating temporarily in characteristics usually confined to the other sex – is part of what made masochism into a perversion. Feminine masochism was not considered abnormal.

Times have changed; many women no longer uncritically play out the traditional roles allotted to them, and both genders, since at least the sixties, have engaged in a kind of creative cross-dressing. Exquisitely dressed youths with long golden hair and earrings are no longer a controversial sight, nor are women with crops and eighteen-hole Doc Marten boots. A revolution in manners and sexual mores means that gender roles are now more fluid, that there's a sense in which each individual customizes their own style from a central pool, with far fewer characteristics being restricted to one sex or the other. Like the kind of travel book in which a writer from abroad describes your own country's quaint customs, contemporary studies of sexual difference may arouse widespread interest because of their promise to tell the reader where it lies, because it is no longer all that clear. More obvious is a growing cultural androgyny.

So the context is different and masochism, once the

province of the man who wanted to enjoy the feeling of being placed in an inferior position, can now be seen as a problem for women, who have repudiated secondary status and striven for equality. Part of the problem is due to monolithic ways of thinking about human behaviour, the assumption that sexual pleasure should be of a piece, just as respectable as the rest of one's actions. There is also the anxious wish to fulfil normative roles.

Women are understandably keen to reject the old claims, which could be interpreted in the sense that we enjoyed the suffering that our subjugation caused us, expressed by the same men who continued to deny us equality. So the idea of masochism as an essential characteristic of women can be rejected as self-serving masculinist propaganda alongside ideas that women make 'good listeners' or other such ready characterizations, as prescriptive as they are descriptive.

The myth can be denied, but what if women really *are* masochistic, in a very generalized sense of the term? If there is a strong wish in women to act counter to their own interests, to embrace suffering, what hope for the future of feminism? It is a question that feminism asks itself, that appears as a kind of limit case, a paradox with no solution. Is masochism our Achilles' heel, the undertow that pulls us back from the brink of equality? Are our endeavours in the outside world defeated as soon as it comes to admitting, for example, to enjoyment of sexual slavery? The suffering that women have embraced, particularly in the past, can be understood as offering some kind of pleasure, even if this is the dubious pleasure of acting the martyr. Looked at from this perspective, perhaps such women were not in fact acting against their own interests at all. There are issues here about what kinds of pleasure are socially valued and what kinds draw down censure, what kinds of pleasure articulate themselves as fully sexual and what kinds deny their erotic content.

There are so many mingled fears and unanalysed associations in this trend of thought that it acts as a sinister, tangled web that spooks feminism. Part of this problem, an important part, is on the level of image: the exemplary feminist is powerful, healthy, with an enlightened self-interest. It is hard to imagine the masochistic woman occupying this role (though as a matter of fact it is more than likely).

The aura of feminism is heroic, whether the admired figure is that of revolutionary Rosa Luxemburg or of a successful yet ethical businesswoman, Anita Roddick of the Body Shop, for example. Masochism sits uneasily with such inflation of role models. There could be a fear that if anything were to upset the process of aspiration, we would be right back where we started, without any rights at all. 'Masochism' can seemingly become synonymous with everything that a woman does or feels that undermines her sense of equality.

Of course, the image is a surface reflection of feminism's real concerns and aspirations. And in some deep sense any form of masochism is going in another direction, down rather than up, into the world of self-annihilation or self-shattering rather than that of self-assertion. But perhaps women could claim that world too, imagine that downside as theirs, live out that part of themselves in a non-reactive, non-paranoid way.

Another way of thinking through the relation of masochism to feminism is through the notion of the shadow. Jung thought that once one's chosen conscious attitudes were in place, there was a kind of coalescence of all the rejected elements, a shadow personality that acted in a compensatory way to the conscious side. The achieving side of feminism excludes important elements that also need satisfaction, casts a shadow that continues to haunt it. The shadow side is ignored at one's peril, because it is important for the psyche and the body, rooted down into the physical realities, whereas the choices one makes for oneself tend to be aimed towards the ideal.

In some ways, their shadow is more present in women's lives than in men's, or less escapable. Women menstruate, give birth to babies, breastfeed, are on the receiving end of the reproductive process in a way that men are not. These biological, nurturing processes require courage, patience and generosity, but there is little recognition of this. The most fundamental aspects of human life are the least visible, as if the entire culture were dominated by some communal vision of a sterile masculine ideal, some bronze statue of a military man.

Wherever feminism promotes female assertion and achievement it unavoidably denies another side to life. Masochism is part of the feminist shadow, containing within it the images and longings that feminism has discarded but that remain strongly and *necessarily* present in women's lives.

In arguing this, I do not assume that feminism has achieved so much that we can now begin to explore the more difficult areas of ourselves as a kind of leisure pursuit, a sort of icing on the cake. What I would like to argue for is an adaptability to context and circumstance, a fluidity that would allow a woman's different (sometimes contradictory) facets to be expressed without drawing forth disapproval. I also consider sexual engagement in its many forms as a neglected resource for women, a point of access to self-knowledge and to vital energies. Why should the rich and varied landscape of sexual behaviour remain the province of men, why should we hold back from exploring our own heterogeneous pleasures, remaining in some tight-lipped haven of post-Victorian censoriousness, hardly moving beyond the missionary position?

A normative wing of feminism does mobilize contempt to score points. This perspective sees masochism as self-hatred, and therefore as something from which we should attempt to free ourselves. In this view we are not only oppressed, but that oppression goes so deep that it becomes reinforced in our own negative assessments of our worth. It assumes an unattractive connivance, where women collude in the masculine crushing of themselves and others. The answer is to throw off our chains, by some triumph of the will to remake ourselves in a higher, better mould. The colour and tone of this analysis is close to that of an ascetic left-wing sect, continually probing its members for signs of disaffection, demanding absolute adherence to the cause. A desexualized ideal is placed before us, and contrasted with a denigrated version which we are supposed to recognize and repudiate.

A psychoanalytical version of this view is that sadomasochism represents masculine domination and feminine submission in a pure form. The argument is that the masochist is a woman with a problem: she cannot separate from her mother. This does not mean that she is to be found still living at the parental home, but that she has difficulties in becoming *psychologically* autonomous.

The image here is of a woman who is clinging to the idea of a good, powerful mother, an idea that she protects from destruction by inhibiting her own aggression, which leads her to identify with a sadist instead to get a vicarious sense of power and freedom. Basically, this view of masochism sees it as a kind of substitute for love, as the result of a developmental impasse, a pathology or perversion, something that needs a cure. It is a disapproving, unsympathetic explanation that finds no value in the lived experience of the masochist, that can only promote a rehabilitation into the world of normality.

These perspectives share a common feature: the writers who offer this analysis are not identified with the colluders, the helpless clingers. They divide women into two camps, the submissives and the women warriors, and it is quite clear that they themselves belong to the latter group. What these analysts gloss over is the pervasiveness of masochistic motifs in women's desire. Nancy Friday's compelling collections of women's sexual fantasies show that scenarios of bondage and rape are commonplace. Humiliation and degradation have an important place in women's erotic imaginations. I am not talking about a tiny minority of troubled, unhappy, mother-fixated women suffering from arrested development, if such women exist. Masochistic fantasy is one component of the varied repertoire that many women have recourse to, and any diminishing of that imaginative resource is a blow against us, not in our favour.

Women, like men, tend to be ordinary rather than exceptional, more pragmatic than saintly. And we may often have other things on our minds aside from equality. Equality is a clear-cut republican kind of concept, and not obviously linked to questions of the sexual, or to psychological qualities. Feminism can address much more than these public, quasi-legal issues, can incorporate a far-reaching, risk-taking, inventive aspect.

Some more recent feminist thinking is clear-sighted enough to see the bedroom as an adventure zone just as much as the boardroom. What that leads to is the widening of women's sexual possibilities, a political demand entirely compatible with feminist manifestos. Women's desire is multiple, not singular, and that is something worth exploring, developing and celebrating.

In my view, there should be few constraints as to what defines our best interests where sex is concerned. Ethics and survival should constitute the limits of erotic behaviour, not propriety or normality: consciousnesses need to be lowered rather than raised. Sexual pleasure delights in the ideologically incorrect (though one would not imagine so from reading pornographic magazines, which seem to promote a disappointingly domesticated and predictable view of sex). Master and slave scenarios, chains and whips in the bedroom are completely compatible with membership of Amnesty International. To think otherwise is to claim a false innocence, an ignorance of sex and of the imaginative engagement it demands.

I am not trying to argue that patriarchy has nothing to do with masochism – obviously it does. All inequalities find their way into the fantasy world of sexual domination and submission, lending their particular flavour to the enjoyment to be had from assuming the position of being humiliated, invaded, crushed.

Masochistic pleasure does not merely reflect inequalities and unfairness, however; it *eroticizes* them. What that means is that they are taken out of the general and made into something specific and personal, becoming a kind of possession, for a while, to be rendered tangible, observed, participated in, enjoyed, played out, exhausted. There is also a process of translation at work, a theatrical impulse; a scene of sado-masochistic sex bears little resemblance to actual emotional or physical violence in that the gestures and parts of the body employed are different, and most of all, the relationship between those involved is different. Within consensual sado-masochism there is no place for bullying. The roles may be reversed, or the submissive position may be assumed in an extreme form – either could have an imaginatively transformative or even subversive potential, if one were determined to locate a political statement in such flux.

I would locate political usefulness not in the particular kind of act but in the psychological adaptability and mutual trust of such lovers, who move from a public self through various imaginary, private selves, each enabling the other. The masochistic self is a role waiting to be occupied. Our couple acting out a master-slave fantasy have to negotiate sensitively a shift of identities and a sliding away of their usual ways of speaking, moving around each other, responding to each other's demands. In this secret recess, the man can explore his passivity and narcissism, the woman her lust for power.

Feminism has allowed women the possibility of defining and moving into a position of equality. But if this becomes a monolithic position, denying other imaginative possibilities, then feminism becomes a rigid strait-jacket, and out of touch with the complexities and compensations that women's lives involve.

Those who are most attracted to masochism may be the women whom feminism has served best, whose self-assertion has mostly been achieved. The women who have made it, who are successful in their own eyes, turn to masochism to live out the humiliation, the submission that they no longer have to endure anywhere else, or to remind themselves of other realities.

This book is not some post-feminist tract, but part of a wider attempt to widen women's sphere of action. I would argue that a strong, self-confident, humorous, flexible feminism can incorporate self-contradiction, where a more tremulous, immature version remains fundamentalist and univocal, even oddly self-mutilating.

The Vagina as a Wound

Many of Freud's followers were women, for example Lou Andréas Salomé and Princess Marie Bonaparte, whom he complimented on her virility. The latter, in her book *Female Sexuality*, describes the results of an operation which she herself, along with a number of other women, underwent: it involved removing the clitoris and repositioning it nearer the vagina, in an attempt to attain the much-desired vaginal orgasm. The results were reported as generally successful, except in one case in which the patient 'had only been satisfied twice in normal coitus, and then only while the cut, which became infected, remained unhealed, thus temporarily mobilising the essential feminine masochism'. As novelist Leslie Dick points out, one suspects that this case history was Bonaparte's own.

This rather disturbing case history shows how women have paid high prices – in Bonaparte's case, the cost of two surgical operations plus the loss of a functioning clitoris – to be mutilated and improved in the quest for male-defined versions of normality. It was not that she couldn't have orgasms at all, just that she could only have them when she was on top.

Bonaparte used the term masochism correctly, not to define her hapless attempts to conform to masculine ideals, but to describe the sexual arousal caused when the site of the excision of her clitoris was grazed in intercourse. In one sense only was Bonaparte able to have vaginal orgasms. This is if we follow through the logic of the equation between vagina and wound to be found in Freud, the Surrealists and even contemporary US slang ('gash'). If the wound can also be a vagina, then Bonaparte's surgery did achieve its aims, if only temporarily, while the infected cut had not yet healed.

Passion

Masochism is not officially popular; or rather, few of us are prepared to say that we like it. A defence of it has to begin by pointing out that it is not the property of a few kinky people, that we are all involved at various levels. Also implied is a critique of the concept of normality itself, the extensive network of prohibitions and taboos that preserves a purified image of family life from the challenges of homosexuality, female sexuality and sado-masochism. Human beings are not pure – we tend to be curious about every kind of sexual variation – but fear of being considered outside the norm has us first giving in to fascination and then denying it. It is a classic structure, but it is more than a little hypocritical.

A female social worker becomes involved in a sado-masochistic relationship in which there is no trust between herself (the masochist) and her lover (the sadist). Though she is obsessed by him she feels abused by his lack of concern for her. Finally he finishes the relationship and in revenge, she sets up a scenario in which she pretends to have been violently raped so as to have him arrested by the police. This is the plot of Jenny Diski's novel *Nothing Natural*. It works on a similar level to the titillating stories of sex abuse published in the tabloids: the enjoyment of reading exact and intimate details of sexual contact accompanies a paranoid distancing of the reader from conscious pleasure by identification, in Diski's case by the vengeful ending which discredits both of the lovers as somehow pathological.

It is a pity, because the earlier part of the novel gives a convincing picture of the intensities of this particular kind of love, the combination of resentment and physical longing, even of a kind of infantile bonding. Descriptions like this are rare.

Longing belongs to women as much as it does to men, if not more. Here I want to look at a kind of counter-culture, a culture that acts as a counterpoint and refuge from modernity's pervasively gung-ho, superhero values. And I want to challenge the view that women need to identify with the latter set of values if we are to claim an authentic voice.

There are other kinds of feminine voice. Women sing exquisitely about the kind of damage that love brings with it, from Billie Holiday to Marianne Faithfull. When Lady sang the blues, telling of lovers who left her or beat her or had other women, she evoked a harsh poetry of drug dependency and her voice held within it a despair of racial oppression. And in Faithfull's song 'Broken English', her voice is trembling, crushed, broken, but pure and untouchable. The masochistic voice is poignant, expressing the pathos of what women suffer at the hands of men, not as complaint or as celebration, just as a deep, soulful kind of truth to experience. These songs are about passionate love, the kind that has nothing to do with having a mutual interest in scuba-diving and everything to do with obsessional longing.

This kind of brooding passion fixes on the specific qualities of the other: the inflections of his voice, his manner of stooping slightly, the special way he has of drinking a cup of coffee. Masochistic love is very much interested in the person of the other, but not all that much in the other as a person. There is some kind of sadness in it right from the start, a sense that the beloved will not always be around, an intensity that fixes on each physical attribute or perceived quality and makes it into a monument. In some sense this kind of lover does not fully believe in the reality of the other, expects them to disappear suddenly or treats them like a photograph, a representation of something that is already in the past. The masochistic lover is in mourning even though the beloved is not dead. And since it is not much fun playing a corpse, taking up a masochistic position in love often means precipitating the demise of the affair or preventing it from ever getting off the ground. Which, one might suspect, is exactly what the masochist somehow wants, in spite of all her protestations of undying devotion.

I surmise, then, that one characteristic of this kind of wounded love is a desire for solitude, masquerading as an addiction to suffering. By taking up a position of excessive humility, a woman who loves a hurtful or indifferent man may manage to preserve her own space and autonomy, rather like a nun who 'marries' Christ instead of an ordinary man. The solitude involved may not be simply about being on one's own, but about relating to the other person from a fixed, immovable point, projecting on to them one's own fascinations or bringing them into an existing imaginary landscape rather than engaging with them reciprocally, being open to and inhabited by the other's fantasy worlds. This behaviour is not to be classed as a disorder, however, even if such unrequited adoration actually prevents the development of reciprocity. It may be the shape of first love, or of kinds of love that only occur at particular moments and are not the less valuable for that.

Is masochistic love, though, so very separable from the everyday variety? Or is it a sublime version of the ordinary story, is it a kind of art? The word 'passion' expresses the quality of masochistic love, referring as it does to the story of Christ's Passion, his suffering at the hands of his torturers that is illustrated in Roman Catholic churches in the twelve stations of the cross. Passion involves the extremity of physical sensation – in the Christ story, the crowning with thorns, the dragging along of a too-heavy cross upon which he is to be crucified – like the weight of a life that can be experienced as a burden, a painful road to a pitiable death.

It may be considered depressive, then, from a psychological standpoint. Masochistic devotion can be seen to involve a quality of sadness, a sense of the harshness of existence and its transitoriness, the kind of quality one hears in the songs of the composer John Dowland, for example, or the numerous *leçons de ténèbres* of Baroque music, or poetic essays like the metaphysical *Cypress Grove* by William Drummond. The sense of stillness and dark depths that echoes in such seventeenth-century music and literature requires an inwardness that might now be called depressive, and that has much in common with a developed masochistic sensibility. It seems to me that psychology (in which I include psychoanalysis) has understood very little about passion. The cultural heritage from which we learn about it is older and has a quality of grace entirely lacking there.

Psychoanalysis has as its aim, articulated perhaps tongue-in-cheek by Freud, of bringing the analysand to a state of ordinary, everyday unhappiness. The idea is intentionally prosaic, cutting down to size those people who might rather suffer occasionally but sublimely. He is reducing their pretensions and reminding them of their own erotic investment in such suffering. It is as if Freud were proposing a general symbolism around the need to suffer, proposing to even out individual, personal, precisely evolved patterns of behaviour and replace them with a ready-made set that would do for all. We would all suffer more or less similarly, more or less to the same degree. Nothing could be less passionate.

I have suggested that masochistic love is passionate, sad and somehow solitary, rather than affectionate, engaging and joyful. One could decry it by describing it as infatuation, but that would be to deny its seriousness and emotional value. A woman who seeks out this situation may do so for particular reasons, at particular times. One of these times is when there is a process of mourning at work.

An example of this is in Marguerite Duras' *La Douleur*, an autobiographical piece set at the end of the Second World War. Marguerite's husband, Robert L, has been discovered by a resistance fighter (French former president François Mitterrand, in fact) in one of the concentration camps, but he is so emaciated as to be virtually unrecognizable, his chances of survival minimal. The masochism of the narrative lies in Marguerite's erotic identification with Robert, her compulsive imitation of the dying man. As she waits for him, not knowing if he is alive or dead, she pours her energy into vicariously experiencing his suffering, continually fantasizing about his death, dying with him. 'Bursts of machine-gun fire every minute inside your head. And yet you're still there, the bullets aren't fatal. Shot in transit. Dead with an empty stomach. His hunger wheels around in your head like a vulture.'

She falls apart physically, cannot move, work or sleep, is continually ill with fever, and shuts herself up in her flat alone so that she can join Robert in the black ditch where she imagines him dying. She dwells on the imagined details of his corpse lying with feet in the air, swarmed over by vermin, open to the sun and rain. 'Perhaps he's already been dead for two weeks, lying peacefully in a black ditch. Already vermin are crawling over him, swarming inside him. A bullet in the back of the neck? In the heart? Between the eyes?'

Robert is brought home, a living skeleton, a literal death's head, and the process of helping to nurture him back to health reveals what is really at stake in Marguerite's vicarious participation. 'I start to eat again too, and to sleep. I put on some weight. We're going to live. Like him I haven't been able to eat for seventeen days. Like him I haven't slept for seventeen days . . .'

What is revealed only at this point in the narrative is that Marguerite had other losses before the imagined loss of Robert. Even before he was captured she was in a state of overwhelming bereavement. 'When I lost my younger brother and my baby I lost pain too. It was without an object, so to speak: it was built on the past. But now there is hope, and pain is implanted in hope.'

These losses had been so devastating that they had never been fully lived through or comprehended. The eroticizing of the maimed, utterly vulnerable figure of Robert enables Marguerite to access her suffering and direct it again into the world and reverse the process. From an insensate, numbed state she moves through painful participation and out into a renewed femininity. At the end of the narrative we encounter a quite different Marguerite, who is on holiday with a group of friends, including the now healthy Robert, and she is shown as a woman who simply and calmly inhabits her body. Her masochism has been a means of bringing sensation back to a despair, through a kind of desperate, obsessive eroticizing of morbidity.

It is no accident that the emaciated figure of Robert is a reminder of the crucified Christ. The narrative of *La Douleur* works because it is one of redemption, of hope implanted in suffering, in contrast to the out-and-out unrelieved misery that Marguerite had been unable to make into any kind of story, and hence never got over. The dramatic story of a man brought back from death's door at Auschwitz actually carries the force of the other losses with it, allowing the deadened feeling to move back into life. The masochistic process of a symbolic death is experienced to the physical and emotional extreme only because redemption is on the cards; it is a calculated risk and in no way a mere capitulation to external forces.

This kind of masochistic narrative always contains a grain of hope, the sense that an ordeal gone through results in a renewal, a recharging of batteries. Surely that is quite different, then, from a hopeless melancholic kind of love for a bad, violent or unattainable man? Yet even that enables an exploration of feeling for its own sake and its own value, as opposed to apathy or emotional paralysis.

Duras' story shows how healing masochism can be, precisely because it can bring an existing state of inarticulate suffering into contact with what is usually considered to be its opposite, an erotic investment. This would be one distinct argument in defence of masochism. But just to go a little further, the question arises as to how this coming together of antagonistic sensations could possibly happen. Bodily experiences don't fit with the language of sensory opposites; this simple conceptual model seems unequal to its task. Many writings on masochism cite its paradoxical nature, its reconciling of apparently incompatible categories, pleasure and pain. But if the two sensations can be fused together, one might suspect that they are not in such an obvious opposition as it has been thought. Perhaps, for example, they are both variants on the same theme, that of feeling. What operates in *La Douleur* is a different kind of binarism, between unfeeling and feeling. This is an important clue to understanding masochism both as a sexual and a creative or cultural phenomenon.

Feeling, excessive response – we have found ourselves on

that same ground again, back with Bill Viola and his reading of Bergson, with Bersani and his reading of Freud, with my own formulation, derived from both: masochism protects you from your engulfing fear of the entire universe by encouraging one part of it to invade you and ravish you. Virginia Woolf in *Moments of Being* talks of her incapacity to block out thoughts, images, sensations. The dangers of such oversensitivity are that one is laid open to the elements, liable to be overwhelmed by huge levels of stimuli. A constitutionally masochistic sensibility lacks some sort of protective mental sheath that reduces sensation to a bearable level. In Woolf, though it is unlikely that she made the connection consciously, everything is erotic, from the sound of the acorn trailing along the floor to the doodles glimpsed in the margin of a notebook. Those who look for copulation in Woolf's novels are left disappointed, but their language is richly and openly sensual, receptive to voices, light and dark, the sea, snails and birds, every sensory stimulus.

The opposite number to a constitutional masochist is someone who would depend on excessive amounts of stimuli to become aroused. Though contemporary, consensual sadists don't fit this description, Sade himself probably did, and the incredible menus he ordered while incarcerated in the Bastille certainly bear witness to his gluttonous appetencies.

I referred earlier to the sense of jadedness, the over-satisfying of desire that chokes up one's enjoyment of everyday life. It seems to me that there are other kinds of states that result in such apathy or disaffection, though they may be quite different in other ways. The numbness of Marguerite in *La Douleur* is one of them, a spiritual paralysis that results from an inconceivable and incommensurable loss. Another may simply be the dulling of habit and routine. Masochism in this context is not so much about bringing pleasure to an existing suffering but about bringing sensation to a state of unfeeling.

63

The constitutional masochist, as I have termed the kind of person Virginia Woolf describes herself as being, may find life so shattering as to need a lot of protection. Professionally he or she would be limited, unable to cope with pecking orders and the push and shove of working life. Such people do frequently become artists – musicians, sculptors, poets – exploiting their heightened level of experience to bring insight to the rest of the world. But there isn't any reason to think that one gender is more or less constitutionally masochistic than the other.

I have been trying to show that women may eroticize their suffering or love obsessively for all sorts of good reasons, rather than because they are unaware or unreformed. Sometimes there is a need to love without being loved, because one has not fully detached oneself from a previous lover or because ultimately one wants to preserve one's autonomy. Or even because one needs to accept pain from someone who is loved rather than suffer inarticulately and impersonally. This kind of love can be a way of changing depression into sadness, an unfocused greyness into the pure black of a winter night.

I want to repeat that this book does not defend any kind of abuse of women by men, any forced sex or violence. It is not a question of treading a fine line, because the line is clear and heavily marked, but of the qualitative difference between the subjugated victim and the erotic adventuress. In a male-dominated society, few women have entirely escaped membership of the first category. That is one compelling reason why we need to rewrite, rework, *reverse* past narratives for our own purposeful pleasures. It is an important way of accepting and integrating vulnerabilities rather than denying and taking flight from them.

The reclaiming of masochism would be analogous to gay men reclaiming the word 'queer', for example, or lesbians the word 'dyke'. It is precisely where something denigrates or harms that it needs to be taken on and owned, worked on and transformed. I have heard a group of feminist psychoanalysts suggesting that lesbian writer Pat Califia was into sado-masochism because her stepfather beat her; her sexual practices, they suggested, were a pathological attempt at mastery.

But S/M practices are nothing like real violence – nobody is beaten up, for example, there is no question of a *repetition* of the original scene. In consensual sado-masochism the idea is to control pain for sexual purposes, to stop when it goes beyond that limit. To equate the two is like comparing traffic noise to a sonata. On the contrary, Califia, like many women who have been the target of male violence, is dramatizing it for her own purposes, rewriting oppression as pleasure, and using it to have a great sex life.

The Story of *The Story of O*

So far I have argued that masochism requires agreement from the participants. There is something straightforward about this, something that should, for example, be used in law to distinguish masochistic practices from abusive ones, in which consent is lacking. Masochistic sexual practices to which the adult parties have consented, and which cause no lasting bodily harm, ought to be considered ethical and legal, while abuse of non-consenting or underage partners is indefensible. The difference is quite clear, and is comparable to the difference between sex and rape.

The worry might be that things can get 'out of control', that something about S/M sex is obsessional, that it is an addiction to sexual violence that snowballs, only to end in real bodily harm to one or more partners. I know of no evidence for this, except the sad case of a Conservative MP who caused his own death through a secret ritual, a solo act whose risks he misjudged. There may be myriad people who engage in these kinds of activities: in general, this book is concerned with what happens between two people, the masochism derived from Sacher-Masoch, rather than singular pleasures. What I am saying is that the idea of masochism as a compulsive, auto-destructive behaviour is rather more fearful than it is persuasive or explanatory.

I should add that the idea of self-destructiveness seems to me to paste over more than it explains. For example, subcultures that perform rituals of skin piercing or 'scarification' and whose members wear bondage clothing tend to come in for this kind of labelling, where the Sunday supplement reporter classically signals his or her own unease and distance in a marked fashion while serving up the details for the vicarious titillation of the readers. Yet tribal societies perform such activities communally through rites of passage. These are understood as ceremonies with symbolic importance in which the participants show their self-control while undergoing knife cuts, muscle piercing, even branding. When in Western societies people mutilate themselves individually, it could be interpreted, for example, as a wish to concretize an emotion or to let out bad blood or to mark a particular event on the body, none of which would be pathological. Indeed demonization of such activities testifies to a fear of physical experience, a generalized uptightness.

S/M, consensual sado-masochism, is essentially in the service of masochism rather than sadism. Sade's victims do not agree to their tortures and mutilations – if they did they would cease to fulfil their role. The masochist cannot impose himself by force; the true sadist must.

Is there not a grey area in which the question of power comes into play? Power may bewitch and fascinate, crude force may hold in thrall. An aura of manly power may be all that is needed to evoke feminine masochism, indeed the domination of masculinity as an order itself may be the object of such worship. One way of getting into the centre of the controversy such observations tend to arouse is to look at a specific example, of a post-war French novel which seems at first sight to play into the hands of masculinism, a novel hardly less scandalous today than when it first came out in 1954. In this novel we encounter the figure of a woman adoring the male and offering him her unconditional love and allegiance.

The Story of O was written under the pseudonym of Pauline Réage, and the identity of the author was to remain a secret for four decades. *Histoire d'O*, first published in Paris, is undoubtedly a shocking book, especially when read from within an Anglophone context unused to the extremities of French eroticism – as reading Sade for the first time comes as a shock when one contrasts it to the comic, bawdy and comparatively gentle tradition of English libertinism from Rochester to Cleland.

In this pornographic fantasy, a young woman, O, is blindfolded and abducted by her lover René to a castle where she is turned into a slave and the sexual object of a group of young men. She is whipped, chained and violated, her anus gradually being enlarged so as to serve her masters' sexual proclivities better. All this is done with her consent – she allows it for the love for René. But the process he asks her to undergo changes her feelings for him, as if she were coming to worship raw masculine force, the ferocious order of virility itself, and when he hands her over to an older, more powerful man, an English aristocrat, she finds that her love has also migrated. The torture and submission then intensify to the point where O's buttocks are branded with a special sign of Sir Stephen's, while her labia are pierced and rings with his mark inserted in them.

What sort of person would write a book like that? In August 1994 the front cover of the *New Yorker* announced the unmasking of the author of the novel, creating the literary media sensation of that year. Inside was a photograph showing the figure of a frail but rather beautiful elderly lady standing outside the publishing offices of Gallimard (where she worked as an editor and translator for most of her life). This was Dominique Aury, the author – not unmasked at all, she had simply decided, finally, aged eighty-six, to tell. It was not as if nobody knew – in fact, the people who did know even included a one-time Minister of Justice, according to the article – but the rumours about the authorship had nevertheless continued to proliferate, and strikingly, all the candidates were men. That such a book could be written was only mildly controversial within the Parisian context; that it was written by a woman, however, seems to have been considered hardly thinkable.

As John St Jorré pointed out in his article, this was the first explicitly erotic novel to be written by a woman in the modern era. For this reason alone it is a cultural landmark, the first moment that a woman writes a specifically feminine sexual fantasy, even if anonymously. One would hope to find there some grain of truth about women's sexuality, something that would mark this book out from those written by men attempting to inhabit the skin of their female protagonists; and in my view there is something that rings true, it is an honest statement about desire, not just rehashed male fantasy.

What sort of person was Dominique Aury? First of all, anonymous – doubly so since that name, too, was one that the author had assumed during the Second World War, when she worked in the Resistance. Her real name is still unpublished. She was a woman in love; *The Story of O* was originally written for the purpose of fascinating her lover Jean Paulhan, the editor of an important literary review, who she knew liked the work of Sade. It was his efforts that resulted in the novel's publication. (Paulhan was a kind of king-maker who, for example, also first published the controversial writings of avant-garde poet Antonin Artaud.) And she was as highbrow a literary figure as you might come across, translating difficult works by the seventeenth-century religious author Sir Thomas Browne, working on a collection of French poetry and writing numerous learned articles alongside her editing career. These credentials were not lost in the production of *The Story of O*, which was written with a pure, limpid prose style that drew forth praise from distinguished French writers when the novel first appeared. André Pieyre de Mandiargues, for example, writing in the literary journal *Critique*, applauded the book as a *'roman veritable'*, one of only two or three since the works of Proust, and thought that Réage would now enter 'this small society of the accursed and the happy that is the only aristocracy one can still consider with a certain respect'.

The book emerged, then, from a context of obscurity, anonymity, passion, secrecy, from a feminine and literary space. It was the work of a sophisticated intellectual. Like Sacher-Masoch's *Venus in Furs*, it was intricately woven into a real-life affair, far from being a product aimed at a market: Dominique Aury wrote her fantasy down with a soft pencil in a notebook alone at night, exploring the darker recesses of her soul in the hope of binding her lover to her. Does that intention negate the authenticity of the book, in that she was merely reflecting Paulhan's own Sadean preoccupations from the position of the victim? The secluded castle at Roissy, the group of cynical male libertines, the numerous subjected women, are self-conscious references to recurrent motifs in Sade. One major difference is that this is a love story, that O goes through all the subjection for the sake of love, that she is consenting. The reason for her consent is her desire to belong to the man she loves.

In other words, O participates in a process of cruelty stoically endured in order to belong, body and soul, to another. It is a cumulative denial of the self that entails enormous self-discipline, a kind of perverse, passionate ascesis. The contrast between the O of the novel's beginning, a successful fashion photographer wearing a suit with a silk blouse, who is out walking in one of the Paris parks with her lover, and the woman at the end of the book, wearing an owl-mask that covers her whole head (possibly another reference, in this case to a painting by Max Ernst), otherwise completely nude and attached by a labial ring to a leash, could hardly be more striking. 'The chain, similar to the kind used for dogs – it was that kind – was some four or five feet long, and ended in a leather loop. Once again O donned her owl-mask; and Sir Stephen told Nathalie to take the loop of the leash and walk about the room.'

Despite the horror, or because of it, such images are powerfully compelling. Aury herself has described her nocturnal fantasies as beneficent and protective, perhaps because of the erotic nature of the fantasy, or because of the simple fact that it is a story, something that can be told, a story of an ordeal suffered for love.

There is a particularly crass way of interpreting *The Story of O*, and that is precisely the way that Jean Paulhan, the important French editor and Aury's much-adulated lover, interprets it in a postscript to the novel. It is to say that the book shows a woman admitting to the fact that we really love to be submitted to the dominance of men: 'They have got incessantly to be fed, incessantly to be washed and burdened, incessantly beaten.' This misprision shows once again the gulf between the sadist and the masochist. Paulhan's preface to the book glibly repeats Nietzsche's exhortation to his assumed male reader to visit a woman with a whip in one hand, and gleefully insists that here is a woman admitting to the essential secret of women: they like their subjugation, they love to be confined to the home, sewing, etc. At the same time, Paulhan cannot help noticing the fanaticism, the fierce intensity of the novel, and that there is something of the knight, the crusader, in the work's author.

The conflation of an ordinary, everyday, conventional sub-jugation with a fantastic ordeal of torture and mutilation suffered in the name of intense love, seems to arise from what I interpret as Paulhan's cowardice in the face of such an extreme statement of passion. He reduces O's ordeal to a banal anti-feminist posture.

There are elements in this supposed love letter that disturb him, too – more prudish than he would like to admit, Paulhan is disturbed by O's prostitution at Roissy. Aury's fantasies were not just masochistic but polygamous. Though she certainly seems to have tried to intuit his desires, to deploy them within the fabric of her own projections, the enterprise remained the work of her particular imagination.

It is as if the crusading knight's courage had to be turned inward, the ordeal sexualized and profaned, in O. The acceptance of Sir Stephen's mark, for example, is a version of the knight's wearing of his lady's colours. O, like the knight, needs to belong, to devote herself to another. She only needs Sir Stephen so as not to belong to herself. The consent to self-abasement to such an extreme level is accompanied by the transferring of gratification from one level of the psyche to another. At the start of the novel, O has everything she wants, and there is only one thing left to want, which is to deprive herself of it. As the offspring of wealthy parents may join ascetic religious sects in what seems (to those parents, who perhaps had to strive for their money) an incomprehensible rejection of worldliness, O puts herself at the tender mercies of the Roissy libertines.

It is a man's world, according to the soul singer James Brown and a few other people, and masculinity is something to submit to, an obvious possibility. But O's form of submission is quite out of the ordinary; anything but conventional pragmatism, it is a personal decision, a self-abnegation that needs another agency to reinforce it. Yet this makes it sound too self-conscious, not carnal enough. O is burning with sexual desire. When René tells her she isn't opening her legs wide enough, she hears the words with 'a kind of inward prostration, of sacred submission, as if they had emanated from a god, not from him'.

It is not that René is a god, but that he represents a particular order beyond his individuality. As Severin in *Venus in Furs* needed Wanda to fulfil his needs, so O needs masculinity, any man and every man. That is why she is prostituted. *The Story of O* involves an ordeal by which O becomes affiliated to the order of masculinity, and this is achieved before the novel ends, with her beginning to act as a kind of procurer of other women for the male libertines.

Submission as a sexual desire is not gender-specific, it is a possibility for both sexes. And although men and women have different relations to authority or a social level of domination, which can be and are played out erotically, it does seem that the desire to submit is a fundamental human one that crosses other differences. In submission, one is done to rather than doing, and in sexual submission one is done to by somebody who is exciting and attractive. The mind takes a rest while the body becomes simply a receiver of pain and pleasure. The therapeutic implications seem as distinct as the erotic ones.

The *New Yorker*'s exposé resulted in a rash of articles in the media, with the British response tending to be one of castigation of the author for a presumed self-loathing. My view is that this gifted and resourceful woman expressed a fantasy of distinct spiritual and psychological value, a dream of another self, part slave, part animal, from a nocturnal underworld beneath the vitalism of the diurnal self. That such fantasies were beneficent, through the sense of contact with a shadow universe, with the universal realities of life and death, imaginatively rewrought into power and subjection, is something I can at least begin to comprehend. It is to do with letting oneself go, in the full meaning of the term. This is what is needed when you feel stale and stifled in yourself, and desensitized towards others. An ascetic ordeal can claw off this rubber or scale, can reinvigorate the sensitivity of the skin, which may be why masochism so often involves symbolic kinds of flaying, in the form of whipping or cutting the skin.

It may be that masculinity has not had to impose itself as a dominant order as much as one might imagine. This is not, of course, for the reason that Paulhan gives, that women like subjugation. Rather it is that women have sometimes resourcefully exploited a subjected status to fulfil certain needs, that male dominance became a convenient, albeit contingent agency for this self-discipline.

It may even be that women have understood what it is to be feminine in such terms, have found their way to a more marked sense of femininity through this kind of willed submission. Female asceticism in the service of men is, in fact, widespread in the form of dieting and under-eating to achieve a slight body shape that suggests fragility and timidity. This is a strange counterpoint to the outgoing, upfront kind of image that young women's magazines now promote. A self-willed submission – a physical submission, since fasting is a bodily practice and one which literally diminishes the body size – to masculine dominance coexists with a desire for self-determination that makes the former inadmissible. The value of Aury's novel is its honesty about the feminine wish to mark an allegiance to masculinity through ascetic practices.

Masculine power has been at least partly the result of feminine projection. It is true that many women seem to have persuaded themselves to believe in their projections, have endowed their husbands and fathers with the most amazing prestige, the most fantastic levels of power and potency. Yet what was essential in this was the need for something or someone greater than oneself, to which one could offer allegiance.

73

Such women have been in thrall to an idea or an aura rather than to a man of flesh and blood, a creature of need, habit and vulnerability.

The division of not just labour, but psychological and creative potential, between the sexes – men free and outgoing, women sympathetic and compassionate – has proven uncomfortable for many members of both. But even if a more fluid set of gender variables can be achieved, women will, I think, continue to fast, to discipline themselves with exercise, to pierce their bodies and perform a range of other ascetic practices. In this way the significance of masculinity, the fact of male power, is recognized and marked on the body.

There is also a long tradition of masculine asceticism in the service of women, even if today that tradition strikes us as quite out of tune with the historical moment. It is the tradition of the first half of the medieval *Romance of the Rose*, by Guillaume de Lorris, rather than the earthy, comic second half, by Jean de Meun. It is represented by the eighteenth-century man of feeling, by the pre-Raphaelite painters, by writers like Henry James. But the twentieth century tried to put an end to all that, and partially, temporarily, succeeded.

4 The Fierce Order of Virility

On His Bended Knees

Masochism seems to draw down an unequivocal scorn in a way that other human tendencies rarely do. Yet if pressed, most people are prepared to admit to a little masochistic desire. An architect I knew told me how terrified but magnetized he had been by a colleague, another architect, at his workplace who walked forcefully, stomping dynamically along the corridor. The two ended up having a passionate and turbulent affair. An extremely bright woman friend told me she could only desire men who dominated her intellectually. She got what she wanted, too.

Why should something so seemingly widespread be the subject of such disgust? There are at least two reasons for the quality of loathing that masochism evokes, one of them its link to the literally sordid, and the other its ironical abasement of both partners. Both aspects are involved in the human necessity that masochism holds within it, to remind oneself of the lower aspects of existence, the level of soil. The transgressive move here is to mix up this need with questions of love, which is seen through rose-coloured spectacles as being at the opposite end of the spectrum.

In a poem entitled 'The Game', written by an unnamed prostitute in the sixties, the clients and their demands are characterized in an increasingly unflattering way, but the poet reserves her most damning and final indictment for the slave, whose behaviour only needs to be described to evoke the reader's answering sentiments:

> On bended knee he'll crave
> To be allowed to clean your lavatory,
> And when you've stripped him
> And whipped him
> Mercilessly,
> Asks: Do you get many like me?

The reference to the bended knee shows how the masochistic client expresses himself exorbitantly, in a kind of grotesque parody of courtly love, one not directed towards the higher impulses at all, but towards the lower ones, the vile excretory functions of the lavatory. The kind of masochistic behaviour described here is of the most schematic order, as crudely minimal as anything classified by sexology.

Prostitutes are not allowed to pick and choose among their potential clients, the transgression of which law in Jean-Luc Godard's film *Vivre sa Vie* leads directly to Anna Karina's death at the hands of her employers. Do they usually feel this combination of incomprehension and revulsion? An ex-prostitute I know once told me that her feelings were indifferent rather than contemptuous. The call-girl has to put up a screen between herself and the client, to act out a part, because any emotional investment runs counter to her business interests. But the masochistic client in the poem above has drawn some sort of reaction, even if it is scorn.

Why should it be that masochists are so unpopular? What is it that is so disgusting about the demand for cruelty? At least a part of this is due to the kind of unbalanced relationship that is set up between the two people involved. (I will confine myself to thinking in terms of a couple, since it is in this kind of intimacy that masochism seems to flourish, although it is obviously not restricted to two people any more than straight, 'normal' sexuality is.)

It is as if the initial self-abasement, being parodic, disrupts all potential for worth or value, bringing the whole order of things crashing down to ground level. By kneeling in front of the prostitute – in ironic inflection of the gesture of the perfect gentle knight in front of the beautiful, virtuous lady – what the masochist does is disgracefully to tell her just how much of a prostitute she really is, and how very low-grade a client he is. He not only soils himself by lowering himself, but he lowers her, too, by emphasizing how her trade is the inverse phenomenon to the high kind of passion that he invokes. He brings this filth with him, makes sure that she knows he is covered with it by cleaning the toilet, and then demands the inevitable purificatory whipping, which may be done with some gusto given the hostility he has aroused in her.

The masochistic client likes himself well enough to embrace his supposed perversion, likes himself well enough to undergo being despised. As to whether that constitutes real self-valuation, it is hard to say. The annoyance that he evokes reminds us of conversational bores, who though they are prepared to impose themselves and their endless opinions upon you, do not convince you any the more that they value their own utterances or are interested in communicating them. If they were, they would not be boring. Similarly, in the guise of looking for an encounter, someone who pays for cruelty merely projects his own need. Yet differently, in that he is prepared – with a special kind of bravado – to take on an unpleasant, undignified persona, one that makes him almost subhuman. If we think he is a worm, it is because he reminds us of the wormy parts of ourselves. One can only conclude that, enjoying the humiliation of his position, he at some level shows how little he cares what other people think, how little his ball game affects anyone else's. A complete egomaniac – is that the explanation?

It may go a long way to explaining how the client survives the contempt of the prostitute, but what I am concerned with here is that contempt. What the masochist does cannot merely be understood in restricted terms as applying to himself; it actually puts something into circulation, it is a move in the human 'game'. It contributes to a general lowering – there is no other way of putting it – to the level of filth. Dirt, of course, is an incredibly productive medium, which sustains all forms of life, but it is also composed of all the residues of our own bodies, the murky depths of our memories, the opaque things that escape our ideals, everything that is corrupt and mixed. We do not pay tribute to dirt, except in such activities as pottery or gardening (gardeners are perhaps the only people who think well of worms), and there it is only its productive form that we emphasize. The masochist, whether paying or not, however, does pay tribute to dirt, in his own inimitable way. He reminds us of it, and for a reason.

There is a place where our spit lands, where our dirty dishwater arrives, where everything that is no longer needed, everything that's unwanted, indeed all that we want to just dump and forget, has to go. We only imagine such detritus as leaving us with the utmost momentum. We want it underground; we even want to find ways of rethinking all our rubbish as something else so that we do not have to recognize its utter confusion and mixture, hence the success of ecological perspectives and practices such as recycling, which conceptually turn this effluence into something useful.

In the Middle Ages it was common to see death represented in the form of a rotting corpse. I have seen one medieval painting which showed three corpses at three different stages of decay, a stomach-turning image for the modern viewer. Death has undergone a kind of conceptual purification along with many other physical processes that arouse feelings of horror. Doubtless most readers will consider this a positive development. Yet the cult success of films like *Return of the Living Dead*, the popularity of vampire films where Count Dracula steps out of his coffin and where the dead return to full-blooded, vengeful life, seems a signal that the purification of death has been only partly successful. We have not quite been able to forget that at the end of the line we become a decaying, vermin-infested piece of meat.

The horror of dirt and decay, and the success of germ theory, now largely discredited, can be linked to worries about what our own bodies will look like when they are dead, what will happen to them when we're no longer in control. Generalized atheism has removed the soothing belief that death was a transition to another, with God's help better, state of being. Death has become horrible in its sense of unreliability. Chopin wrote his last letter during a fit of coughing that he knew would kill him; in it he asked for his body to be opened after his death, just to ensure that there was no doubt about it and to preclude the possibility that he might be buried alive. He expressed a common fear that one would somehow still be around to witness the proceedings after the death itself, a fear that biology has been unable to remove.

Perhaps the decaying corpses of medieval painting could only be calmly witnessed at that moment in history, when faith was strong enough to withstand the assault of death and decay on the individual, personal body. Our materialism is generally made of more cowardly stuff, though an exception is the work of the late Andrea Fisher: photographs of mutilated war victims that could be icons in a kind of new theology, that give a dignity back to the wasted corpse which has been denied it throughout the modern period.

But the fear and the denial are dominant. Eliot echoes this in *The Waste Land*, in lines taken from Webster. The corpse, planted in a garden, may be ready to sprout and bloom into some unthinkable life, unless disturbed by the sudden frost, or by the dog:

'O keep the Dog far hence, that's friend to men,
  Or with his nails he'll dig it up again!'

Dogs are dirty. They return to their vomit, and to other things, too. The shameless dog digs things up, exhumes corpses, unburies the dead. The dog, man's best friend, is a kind of domesticated, pet version of the Freudian unconscious or the Jungian shadow, the animal side that's always around, that sticks to its master or mistress loyally. Dogs can be comic, and a thoroughly doggy kind of person will make scatological jokes. A fascination with excrement tends to emerge as humour if it wants to be smuggled out into public view.

Scatological preoccupations are now considered more transgressive than sexual ones, if an episode in the film *Trainspotting* is anything to go by. In it, a shy, almost simple boy called Spud goes one night with his attractive girlfriend to her parents' home, where she unsuccessfully attempts to seduce him. Seeing him the next morning at breakfast, her father remarks liberally, 'You have to cut loose sometimes.' The joke is that the looseness applies to Spud's bowels rather than his morals, to which a radically besmirched sheet testifies. The joke defuses the charge of its transgressive, nocturnal material at the same time as it brings it to the light of day.

Masochistic practices may involve humour but they do not go all the way to the joke, however, because that kind of discharge operates too quickly for the kind of disruption that masochism involves to take effect. Its aim is to draw the situation out in a different way, less sniggering, more theatrical. Even the most shameless type of masochist, the user of a sexual service industry, is less self-serving than that.

If masochism is often linked to dirt in some way, if it lowers things to ground level, it arouses a particularly modern form of paranoia, around all the detritus of our living bodies and the meaningless dead thing that each of us will become at some unspecified point. The self-abasement involved in masochism is a *memento mori*, often an unwelcome one. That is one of the reasons why masochists arouse general disdain, in an attempt to counter the undesirable view of an unredeemed mortality.

Most people have endured at least once the uncomfortable experience of being an object of infatuation. To be doted on beyond reason tends to produce the reaction of loathing in the object of devotion. Even when the person who is infatuated is initially perceived as attractive, this impression soon evaporates as their feelings become clear. They arouse in us a feeling of contempt, of scorn, as if a slug were crawling on our flesh. They give us the creeps. All because of their unrequited love for us.

Someone who confirms our attractiveness ought, according to common sense, to be valued for their flattering attitudes, their ego-boosting qualities. But only the most Machiavellian of us actually cultivate them, and even then only so as to draw another, more desired person into the net. Most of us cut the poor unrequited lover dead, as if their existence stifled us, only hoping their affections will be quickly transferred to another person (in which case, there is a slim chance – but only very slim – that one day our desire might eventually fix on them).

Unrequited lovers are instinctively scorned by the very people they need as opposite numbers. Paradoxically, they also need this scorn, to be seen as contemptible, to be put down.

Part of the inequality that is set up by someone who falls into an overvaluation of the desired other person is caused, quite simply, by the fact that the latter has no scope for personal initiative. Rejection is stymied in advance, avoidance is unlikely to succeed, affection is rendered futile, cruelty may be positively welcomed. However the beloved acts, it will only contribute to the further elaboration of the original and uninvited attachment, one that the object is fully aware has no necessary bearing on any intrinsic virtue of his or her own.

One of the myriad things that novels tell us is that courtship is a process whose complexities should never be underestimated on either side. An impulsive love may need to be held prudently in check if it is to be realized in marriage, as Elinor Dashwood in Jane Austen's *Sense and Sensibility* understands and her sister Marianne does not. That is why the first succeeds in her relation to Edward Ferrars while the second fails in her own affair with Willoughby and ends up marrying the Colonel. The emphasis on conduct in Austen novels is ultimately an emphasis on winning; strategic self-reserve derives from the heroine's intellectual scepticism, and her capacity to comprehend and confront the forces of snobbery and veniality arrayed against her.

Of course, there is a difference between the impulsive, ardent lover, who merely overestimates his or her own attractions and is impatient with the vagaries of desire, and the truly infatuated, who knows virtually nothing about the other. But what they both have in common, in varying degrees, is that they arouse discomfort allied to distaste in the person to whom they adhere.

What the masochistic lover tends to do is to cut the appetite of the other person for love or lust. Like the jaded person who has overdosed on pleasure, the object of infatuation feels they have already had too much of something they never imagined having in the first place. Power has been handed over without any demand. There is no role for the imagination.

I have been trying to show how the masochistic client, though seeming to overvalue the object of his attentions, simultaneously brings things down to a sordid level, and how an infatuated lover may create a similar kind of effect, because he or she projects such an obviously glamorized picture of the admired person that the latter is forcefully reminded of their own ordinariness. And the infatuated person, by reducing his or her own worth to nothing through self-abasement, makes those affections not worth having.

When it comes to the sado-masochistic encounter, all of this needs careful strategy. After all, one can imagine another outcome: the desired partner might simply feel depressed, rather than angry and hostile, at the general lowering of worth that the masochist sets in train. Not for nothing, then, is the dominant woman chosen for her strong ego: a weaker one would crumble and reduce the whole thing to a pathetic farce.

Analysing the effect of masochistic love may tell us why it tends to be dysfunctional and even disastrous, but it does not give us much of an idea of what is happening on the inside.

According to a song by Leonard Cohen, there is a war between men and women. Actually, few of us forget this fact. When love attempts to forget about war, it is likely to fail in its aim. But what if failure in love were the whole purpose anyway? After all, love and sex are different, and Severin's name for his predilection is supersensualism, excessive sensuality. The tension that needs to be maintained in sado-masochistic encounters is sexual; it is a temporary bracketing-off of the love relation, an imaginative detour from it.

The masochistic client's genuflection is ironic, but not merely so – what he implies by it is the surrender of one sex to the other, of the order of men to the order of women. This initial and total surrender removes all possibility of a relationship, since only through the negotiations of the courtship ritual could such a relationship emerge. Only the vitiation of all conflict could open the way for the violence that he now demands.

What Do Men Want?

Each sex tends to demand of the other that it carry a few values or personality traits that it wants to keep on the menu, as it were, but does not want to select for itself. It is common to assert that traditional divisions between the sexes have broken down these days, but in fact this is not just a recent phenomenon. Relations between the sexes – or the consensus as to what masculine identity is prepared to include, what it has decided to exclude – have been changing for some time. Women, too, are forging new kinds of feminine identity, throwing out some of the things that were supposedly so characteristic of 'la femme' and taking on some traits previously considered masculine. Here I want to look at how the concept of masochism came into play strategically to prop up a particular kind of masculinity, at the expense of other kinds, and how women were left with the fuzzy end of the lollipop (but only temporarily).

The current state of play in the gender war involves new kinds of terminology to describe roles that have sometimes mutated very slightly, sometimes quite a lot. For example, the adjective 'feisty' has come across the Atlantic and become common currency in Britain to describe the new kind of woman. She is still just as feminine, but also speaks her mind, is not intimidated, may even have a bit of a temper. Helen Mirren in her television-detective role is very feisty indeed. As for the New Man, he cannot decide if he exists at all, and periodically degenerates into the old model, the beer-swilling, football-supporting Lad. Masculine identity is under stress at the moment, and I would guess that many men are not ready to change even if women are now competing for the same ground.

Such linguistic variants are clues to an unease with gender definitions, a sign that they are cracking and something else is trying to get out. But what will emerge is not yet clear.

Before the twentieth century this battleground was being fought quite differently. Society was patriarchal, but men valued themselves as sensitive, feeling people, and as lovers they enjoyed the position of gentlemanly servitude to women. The tradition of the lovely woman seen as imposing upon, holding in thrall the man who delights in his own adulation, goes back to the ancients, when she was described as the 'domina'. In courtly love poetry this theme is the prevailing one. It is not overstating the facts to say that it is central to Western culture's view of itself, given its long-standing importance in literature.

Towards the end of the last century, male thralldom to the desirable woman began taking a distinctly carnal turn, in the late Romanticism of Baudelaire, Swinburne and their contemporaries, including Sacher-Masoch. Here, for example, is a taste of what the educated Victorian would have been reading, from a novel by Swinburne:

> Her perfume thrilled and stung him; he bent down and kissed her feet . . . which he took and pressed down upon his neck. 'Oh! I should like you to tread me to death, darling . . . I wish you would kill me some day; it would be just so jolly to feel you killing me. Not like it? Shouldn't I! You just hurt me and see.' She pinched him so sharply that he laughed and panted with pleasure.

This particular extract is a little comical, and the male character somewhat abject. But the general mood of the times is clearly favourable to the woman being on top. Mario Praz, in his classic study *The Romantic Agony*, shows how in works of that period the woman was presented as not just dominant, but cruel, from Keats's poem 'La Belle Dame Sans Merci' to Flaubert, Gautier and D'Annunzio. (England, according to Praz, was the very fount of what he called 'algolagnia', or the erotic enjoyment of suffering, as well as sadism, *'le vice anglais'*. He asserts that sexual flagellation went on here more frequently than anywhere else.) At the end of the nineteenth century, the angry woman, far from being a feminist heroine, was an icon of depraved, sensual Romantic–Decadent desire.

The great literary tradition, responsible as it is for the task of representing what it is to be human, had as its central and enduring subject the man's passionate surrender to his beloved. From Dante's ordeal in the *Inferno* and the *Purgatorio* in order to be reunited with Beatrice, to John Donne's love poetry, sacrificial masculine love has been a crucial theme. Only in this century has what for many centuries seemed the natural, desirable form of male love been redefined as effeminate perversity, masochism.

The concept of masochism, as I have already said, was only ever intended to apply to men. Smuggled on to the slate of perversions by early sexology in the 1880s, it operated a sly revolution in masculine manners. The accusation it made was that the sacrificial male lover was actually an effeminate pervert. Masculinity emerged in a new light in the subsequent century: it became increasingly and blatantly misogynistic, emotionally inept and homophobic. This formulation of male identity was the one my generation grew up with. The experience of being surrounded by men of this kind was quite probably an important factor in the rapid growth of feminism from the sixties, promoted by more than one generation of disaffected wives and daughters.

In other words, what we think of as traditional male identity, with its explicit demeaning of women, is a fairly recent phenomenon, going back around a century. It was created at a particular point in history when two things were happening. One was that literature was beginning to explore sexuality and redefine love as involving desire, and dangerous desire at that. Sex had in previous centuries, in the Western tradition, been conceived of as merely a kind of rutting, not to be confused with the elevated, spiritual notion of love. It was the stuff of extended jokes, like Chaucer's 'Miller's Tale'. The sexual woman was quite distinct from the revered madonna figure; she might be maligned as a whore or adulteress or presented as a comical figure, the Wife of Bath, to give another Chaucerian example. Men did not expect to respect women of that kind. So the radical late-nineteenth-century move to bring sex – with all its inbuilt conflict and instability – together with what had been a relatively simple matter, love, might have been expected to cause reverberations in terms of men's view of women.

To put it more crudely, from a longer historical perspective, a double standard had operated successfully to keep men generally dominant. Love and marriage were the only things that women were commonly expected to concern themselves with, and in this area alone, men were ready to enjoy secondary status to the desirable woman. If this was the only arena of women's power, at least it was the most central one for society and the family. But modernity fractured this arrangement.

While literary works of the late nineteenth and early twentieth century took the less obvious tack of trying to raise sexuality to a sublime level – as in Lawrence's *Lady Chatterley's Lover*, for example – the broader trend over most of this century has been a deflation of men's worshipping of the madonna figure, and a transformation of love into something that is primarily to do with mating and the reproduction of the species. Women were trying to get off their pedestal and occupy a more wide-ranging position in society. Men simultaneously began to emphasize their virile qualities, and a scientific language that redescribed human interaction in biological terms became popular.

The other, well-documented phenomenon of the late nineteenth century was that women were beginning to speak and write for themselves, so the old contract between the sexes was breaking down. Novelists like George Eliot showed how far-reaching a woman's intellect could be, while Charlotte Brontë described sacrificial love from the woman's perspective in *Jane Eyre*. Women were no longer the blank screens upon which men could project their desires, no longer the mysterious madonna figures who relied on men to articulate their meanings. The stakes had changed; women had started doing the talking.

Masculinity was reconstructed in the mould of the hyper-male, with the term 'gentleman' becoming an archaism. What that meant was a denial of perhaps the most fundamental love relationship between a man and a woman, the mother-child nurturing. An important aspect of the traditional gender contract in which the man exceptionally took on a role of servitude was an implicit recognition of the woman's maternal capacities. With the twentieth-century hyper-male, the woman becomes a plaything or sexual object (remember all those James Bond films with hundreds of disposable Barbie-dolls relegated to serving drinks and dressing scantily?). She is reduced to the level of the pouting, petulant infant.

Men were phallic anti-heroes, denying their own infantile dependencies, unselfconsciously subjugating women. Think, for example, of John Osborne's then-controversial play *Look Back in Anger*, in which women and ironing boards are symbiotically bonded. It has taken half a century for audiences to lose sympathy with his male central character.

The rise of feminism has been a much-needed corrective. Correction, of course, is what the male masochist demands of the woman he admires. In the time of Swinburne and Baudelaire, men may have been attracted to being punished by a woman as a corrective to the prevalent social order in which men dominated. Nowadays one image of feminism could be the dominatrix, dressed in black rubber, who corrects the excesses of reactive masculinism with a whip. An image as clichéd as the seventies hyper-male, one might argue, but perhaps right at this particular historical moment. The dominatrix image used to be restricted to subcultures, was embodied by the lead singer of Siouxsie and the Banshees in late-seventies New Wave music, returned with cone-shaped breasts in the eighties designs of Jean-Paul Gaultier, and now seems to have settled into being a fashion and media staple.

I have tried to show how a special form of masculinity arose over this century and that it is the one we now take for granted. The modern male denied his own fundamental dependencies on women, while surreptitiously satisfying them. He professed no knowledge of homosexual desire and reviled gay men, while addicted to images of buddy bonding in cinematic and televisual culture. His emotional range was limited by his inability truly to fall in love and sensitively experience its passion. Desperate to remain manly, he lost his integrity.

The construction of the term 'masochism' was an important plank in this reformulation of masculinity, characterizing men who continued to enjoy occasional domination by their womenfolk as participating in essentially female characteristics. Men of this kind were now denied their own gender status, not considered men at all, banished alongside homosexuals or 'inverts' to some hermaphroditic hinterland on the borders of humanity.

This narrowing of what it meant to be a man involves a view of normality supported by Darwinist thinking. The notion of human beings as just another species with similar drives, impulses and sexual patterns to the animal kingdom was a major success over this century and has only fairly recently been challenged by post-war French thought. The latter emphasizes the crucial nature of language to our culture, language which separates us from the animal world. Biological thinking reduced women to the level of their reproductive function without respecting the cultural value of the maternal. Men could be considered 'naturally' dominant, though in fact any extensive knowledge of the natural world challenges the use of such terms. (Somehow the sad reproductive relationship of the black widow spider, the female of which species devours the male after the sexual act, tended to be kept out of this picture.)

Those men who have sought to push women back into a

secondary position have had a rough century, all the same. There is no need for me to outline the well-known features of women's emancipation and the extension of women's voices into every area of public debate. The image of the hyper-male is also under duress, not least from the ironic inflection it is given through the borrowing of its postures by an ascendant gay culture: as Darian Leader points out, muscle-bound Arnold Schwarzenegger appears to us as a 'camp caricature of capitalism'.

Are there not other cinematic images of masculinity that are more convincing, though? In the late-fifties film *A Touch of Evil*, Orson Welles plays a cop who is lame, bloated and corrupt yet completely charismatic. His weakness is his envy of the other kind of man, the man who is successful with women, embodied in Charlton Heston, just married to Janet Leigh. At one point Welles is surrounded by a group of his police henchmen when she walks past. They turn away from him, fall silent and watch her pass, glumly hypnotized.

At the end of the film, cheated and betrayed by his best friend, Welles falls into the river; his dead body is grotesque and whale-like. The verdict on him is given by Marlene Dietrich, who says, 'He was some kind of a man.' There is no denying it. There is something about his sheer bulk, his ruthless transgression of the rules, his unredeemed egoism, that is compelling. But Welles is a man for other men, a man's man, although it takes a woman, Dietrich in a black wig, to say it. And most men are just not that good at being bad. Welles's maleness is successful hyperbole, he goes beyond what gender convention requires, it is an unrepressed masculinity that is simultaneously infantile in an almost touching way, which is probably why he loses his battle with the trim, conscientious Heston. The film's subject could be interpreted as masculinity policing its own boundaries. Where the male masochist or the medieval knight is not enough of a man for the modern period, other kinds of man can actually overdo it.

Is male masochism, this time around without the safety net of women's secondary status, an idea whose time has come? Could this culture stop overinvesting terms like 'man' and 'lad' with the implicit differentiation from the supposed threat of femininity? Or is the fear of a rampant, engulfing femininity too great for men ever to relax fully and let down their defences? Is the fear actually about the threat of a matriarchy that would deny men all power, never allowing them to grow up? What do men want?

Some feminist readings of male identity formation do suggest that the problem of male domination is a tough nut to crack. The thesis is that due to the mother's nurturing, the baby, male or female, identifies with her, and the boy later on has the difficult task of changing tack, which he does by rejecting everything female. So adult masculinity is a collection of traits that have been chosen defensively, and while (at least heterosexual) men always seem to feel that they are wanting literal, physical contact with women, they also feel threatened by the eruption of the original identification. In every big man there is a baby girl.

This story seems quite convincing. But I wonder how or when it was decided that men were just the opposite of women? I know this is an abstract kind of question, but why should men have defined themselves as opposite rather than the same? Could the difference be confined to specific acts or gestures or even clothing rather than to the whole gamut of personality? Professor Higgins in the film *My Fair Lady* demanded of Eliza Doolittle, the flower girl, 'Why can't a woman be more like a man?' But the question could be asked the other way around.

In some senses men are on the cultural agenda the way that women were in the debate which took off in the seventies, but which had been simmering for decades before. They have not yet staked their claim, perhaps only half recognizing the opportunity. The potential for a more inclusive, heterogeneous view of what it is to be a man seems distinct, but that vision lacks full articulation at the moment, perhaps still seems a climb-down from the previous incarnation.

In my own utopia, men would have no problem owning up to their masochism, and neither would women. The same people could be assertive and even dominant, things would move rather than remain constricted within gender roles. This utopia wouldn't be free of conflict or even resentment, but it would allow people to inhabit the neglected parts of themselves, to live less fearfully and more interestingly with each other.

And it may even be that some of those characteristics that little boys take on to differentiate themselves from their mothers are worth holding on to, after all. Oscar Wilde suggested that women's tragedy is to become their mothers, men's that they never do. But the disappointments of masculinity are far from overwhelming.

Fascination

Is male voyeurism an invasion of privacy, an aggressive violation of women's personal space? And do the visual arts compulsively re-enact that violation through the way women are systematically positioned in painting, photography and cinema, setting the female form up to be consumed by the male viewer? Is there a rapist-like mentality at work throughout spectatorship of this kind, whether on the level of production or consumption, or is the visual obsession with the female body interpretable in a different way?

In the film *Sliver*, starring Sharon Stone, the owner of a New York apartment block, played by William Baldwin, spends his whole time spying on the inhabitants through a secret bugging system. He has a room with a bank of television screens on which he can watch everything they're up to: bathing, dancing, arguing, having sex. He is one of the suspects in a murder case, and Sharon Stone, who is having an affair with him, becomes understandably worried about this obsession with watching. At the end of the film he is cleared, but she shoots out every one of his screens and as they explode, turns towards the camera and speaks the last words of the film: 'Get a life.' They are obviously addressed just as much to us as to her lover.

The implication is that we are harmless, hopeless cases who should be doing instead of watching. The film has turned on its viewers and started moralizing at us, and the male audience in particular in that men are more identifiable with the William Baldwin character. Having exploited our voyeurism, the film reproaches us for it, exhorting us to action. But what are we supposed to be doing? What sort of life are we supposed to be getting? Is book-editing, which is what the Sharon Stone character does for a living, any more like real life than endlessly watching the screen? Yes, in the sense that it is done for money, for a salary, it is a life, a working life, and that can be contrasted with the moneyed leisure that her lover fills up with the vacuous pleasures of the voyeur. But surely that's not all. The getting of money cannot be the only guarantor that one is acting in the world.

The gender divide implies another critique: while the energetic, modern woman gets on with her life, the man pleasures himself by a kind of gazing that circles around the image of the woman, always coming back to it. Her sphere goes beyond him, and out towards others, but he is cramped in his little world full of television sets, his microcosm; he is limited by his own perversity. Getting a life in this sense would mean adventuring beyond the limits of a compulsive desire, the desire to watch.

The film owes its narrative tension to the idea that this compulsive looking could be linked to murder, the gaze could be sadistic and invasive and perhaps could logically lead to further sexual violence.

That anxiety – that the pleasure of the male gaze is ultimately sadistic – has troubled both men and women over the last couple of decades, especially in areas which deal explicitly with the visual, like film. For example, in the seventies, avantgarde male film-makers avoided images of women altogether for fear of the accusation of scopophilia.

But misogyny seems to go considerably further than the question of the image. And the dangers of this concern when it becomes part of a political agenda are those that any kind of censorship always creates. I mean here the suppression of the work of visual artists, including women, whose work engages with and explores important aspects of women's sexuality: the late Francesca Woodman, for example, whose work investigates the metaphoric potentials of the female body. In one of her photographs she stands naked, holding up her arms, behind a washing-line draped with three tiny furs. The fur both corresponds to and stands in front of the three triangles of hair on her body. Woodman's photographs are narcissistic, fetishistic and sometimes masochistic, saturated with a distinctly feminine eroticism. Yet they have been censured by a wing of feminism unprepared to see them as doing anything other than pandering to exploitative male pleasure.

In the film I have been using as an example, *Sliver*, the propensity for violence and the compulsion to look seem at first to be enmeshed, and it is at this point that Sharon Stone accuses her lover of 'playing God' with his snooping. But the two become separated by the plot when the murderer turns out to be a resident writer, played by Tom Berenger. In fact he is the only other male character on offer for masculine identification. (The writer kills out of envy, not because he hasn't got a life but because everybody else's seems preferable.) One deduces that the anxiety about the male gaze derives from a similar suspicion, namely that male voyeurism is only a small step away from male violence.

This kind of suspicion is really predicated on paranoia, like the slogan that all men are potential rapists. The idea that the man sitting on his sofa with a can of beer watching Marilyn Monroe and Jane Russell in *Gentlemen Prefer Blondes* for the umpteenth time is actually about to get up and slash a couple of women to death in an alley is more than incongruous. It is superstitious.

Even if pornography itself does not result in male violence, it is often asserted that the male look is colonizing and inva-sive. Is there something sinister in the idea of a man who sits comfortably in his protected space enjoying a sense of mastery and ownership of the screen idol who performs seductively, seemingly just for him? Is his gaze homing in on her, fixing her as an object for his sexual desire? Is he vicariously dominating her, positioning her so as to extract the maximum enjoyment from her exhibitionistic role?

This kind of enjoyment is more properly understood as masochistic. The male gaze is not so much sadistic as awe-inspired, fascinated. For the male masochists in the audience, Sharon Stone's challenge is more of an invitation to identify himself not with the envious, vengeful killer of women or the passive stay-at-home hedonist, but with the actress herself. 'Take one more step, male masochists, if you would become true human beings.' Stone herself is the only character who has any real presence. The secret of the male voyeur (and not just in this film) is not his sadism, but his pleasure in a direct identification with the figure of the woman.

In *Sliver* the problem of masculinity comes up again, with the three choices that I have already outlined: the misogynistic hyper-male, the fascinated male masochist and the woman her-self. If the first is a figure who embodies the less acceptable face of the father, the second is easily recognizable as the son, while the woman takes the biscuit by incarnating both daughter and mother. That is certainly the reason that she feels she's got a life.

The challenge of contemporary feminism has gone beyond the critique of the omnipotent male father figure. It is also aimed at the man who cannot grow up, who remains stuck in mother worship, the perennial boy. The way out of these simple positions is the assumption of more complex ones. Sharon Stone's implicit demand is not for men to be just like her, but to be as resourceful as she is, to occupy their own manhood, boyhood and indeed femininity, without fear or confusion.

That seems quite a challenge. If few men are anywhere near getting there, well, probably very few women are as lucky as Sharon Stone, either. But at least it is a step in the right direction.

Disquiet over the pleasure of the image is a very old tradition. In the Old Testament, God forbids Moses to make any graven image in his likeness. During the Reformation, Roman Catholic religious icons were destroyed in waves of Protestant iconoclasm across Northern Europe, since statues and paintings of the saints were considered corrupt, while true faith was thought to soar only in churches deprived of all ornamentation.

Modern debates over visual pleasure may owe some of their intensity to the unresolved nature of this long-standing, hardfought and spiritually crucial issue. The fear is that direct representation – the statue, the painting – steals the thunder, becomes worshipped instead of God and begins to replace him. We may talk about God as a 'he', and thoroughly anthropomorphize him, but it is a step further, it seems suddenly sacrilegious, in the British context, to paint a picture of him as a solidly built, bearded man, in the way that William Blake did.

Yet in Southern Europe it is obvious how much a thoroughly visual Catholicism has to offer both urban and peasant cultures.

The pleasure of the beautiful religious painting or statue is accessible to the poorest peasant working in the heat of the day, and the purity of such enjoyment can hardly be open to question. The culture of images allows a generous, pluralistic religion to involve all of its adherents. Such icons offer a trace of the divine, act as reminders of Bible narratives, simply speak of a plane of experience different from the everyday.

If the pleasurable image is considered sacrilegious in religious cultures that emphasize a strict verticality, it is understandable that even in a post-Christian culture the image of the woman may be considered disturbing. In the Catholic context, the image of the woman is often that of the Madonna, or one of the female saints. In the twentieth-century secular context, images of women's bodies are thoroughly sexualized and often used to sell commodities, used as a kind of currency. As a teenager in a small northern town, I used to walk back from school past a larger-than-life-sized cut-out of a woman in a frilly green bikini outside the camera shop. The distaste that this service industry has evoked is widespread, and one of feminism's finest hours, in my view, was its first sabotaging of the *Miss World* show.

The fragility of a culture that denigrates and mistrusts the image lies in its necessity to keep to a high moral agenda. In a Christian or post-Christian society this means the 'infinite erectness' advocated by Kierkegaard, an uprightness that is not self-righteous but transient and renewable, based not on certainties but on a will to *stay* upright. If the issue begins to be fudged, if evasion creeps in, the pack of cards collapses. Britain's literary, musical and intellectual heritages demonstrate what high principles this culture once aspired to, and in some subcultures still does. But for the most part such strenuous, vertical aspirations have been abandoned, replaced by the horizontal exchange values of capitalism.

What has this meant for the image? A culture that once

97

rejected the representation of divinity, believing in a personal God who was invisible but to whom one had direct access, has lost that central belief and is now susceptible to the flood of every kind of image, good, bad or indifferent.

The image of the woman has become synonymous with a kind of kitsch debasement that is best illustrated through parodic exaggeration in the films of Fellini. Such images curry favour with male consumers while reducing women to two dimensions, to the level of the products they tend to be promoting, whether it is television chat shows or pet food or cars. They also produce an insecurity in women who are forced to see themselves as self-representations, placed in the position of continually projecting themselves, and reviewing themselves as image.

Revulsion from or irritation with the banal representations of women found everywhere in the printed media is a different matter from the issue of male erotic viewing. While the latter is about a kind of stilled fascination, the former is about a tame tickling of male egos. In my view, the flat media images are far more irritating than cinematic impressions of actresses, who move, speak and express themselves through their roles, so are able to move beyond the image.

Someone who watches is not implicated in any true sense. As soon as there is a question of touch, for example, there is a breach of bodily privacy that has had to be fully accepted between the two parties. That isn't true of vision: for example, some people dislike being the object of other people's gaze, while others solicit and enjoy it.

If men surreptitiously enjoy identifying with women, it is visuality that protects them, with its insistence on a physical distance between the viewer and the viewed. The proliferation of images, moving and still, offers us the opportunity to witness a spectrum of events, from sex to violent murder, without feeling implicated. The combination of fascination (I am that person) with freedom (I can see so many varied, exotic things), lassitude (I only have to move my eyes) and distance (none of this is really happening to me) produces an addiction to consumer images. Even a good image cannnot challenge the ultimate fishiness of this form of visuality. Certain art forms do, for instance abstraction, which moves beyond the image into the ungraspable, or conceptualism, which encourages an engagement with the mental and material processes that produce the final image.

Where does that leave the masochistic man? Still trying to get a life, perhaps: still hoping for a closer encounter.

Boy Meets Girl

The image is an important element in masochistic fantasy. Jean Laplanche suggests that having an internal image of being made to suffer by another is an initiating moment in the infant's development of the capacity to fantasize. It is the ability to hold on to such an excessive image inside that begins to produce a sense of interiority in the child. The sense of an inside is involved or enmeshed with the possibility that it may be ruptured, invaded from the outside. This imaginary rupturing is what gives the pleasurable sense that one's inside really exists.

So masochism and the imagination are almost inseparable. We always choose to imagine something that evokes this intensely pleasurable feeling of having something inside, and what does this most strongly is the idea of something *trying to get in*. Perhaps that is one of the reasons that horror films are often about women barring themselves into rooms as monsters or psychopaths batter at the door and window and punch holes through the ceiling.

Visual fascination has been the first move into masochistic fantasy. What happens next is the narrative of the encounter

99

itself. Our adoptive male is almost ready to move on, to take his punishment. But first of all there is some preparing to be done. The scene has to be set, the props wheeled out, costumes put on.

The iconography is typically conceived along the lines of Victorian-style flagellation. But it could also be on a fetishistic sixties note – Velvet Underground's 'Venus in Furs' – the 'shiny boots of leather', the whiplash in the dark.

The costumes are important. For *The Story of O*, Dominique Aury researched eighteenth-century womenswear – crinolines, ruched silk – with a typical academic thoroughness. But the contemporary imagination honours footwear above all: the spiked heels that dig into the back or chest of the supine partner, the pointed toe that may kick or be kissed, or even the soiled shoe that must be cleaned. The cruel partner never wears sensible, practical shoes. Sado-masochism and the wearing of Birkenstock are thoroughly incompatible. These are boots that shine, that may even have spurs, shoes with sharp buckles, tight laces, impossibly high heels, boots that were never meant for walking, except for all over a male masochist.

These shoes are not just an image, though they function well in that sense; they are also likely to be touched, and probably also smelt. (Shoes carry the full weight of the body and are likely to carry a bit of odour, though I wonder if the most committed of foot fetishists could stand the footwear of someone with genuinely smelly feet.) Shoes also carry the identity or role of the person wearing them in a way that no other clothes do. This is why we use the expression, 'If I were in your shoes', and variants of it. Shoes are a mark of social status, so a well-off person is literally well-heeled. People who are interested in clothes know that a pair of shoes is the most crucial element to get right. It crystallizes the whole look more than any other item of clothing. Shoes can edify the wearer through elegance, the sign of luxury. What the masochist knows is that they have quite a difficult job to do, being at the lowest point of the body, the end that is constantly in touch with the ground, in other words: shoes are dirty, they carry metaphoric signs of sexuality in the height of heels, in their tactile qualities. And as we have seen, masochism is all about getting down into the dirt.

The corset, too, is an indispensable garment for gaining the interest of the male masochist. Not since the fifties have women casually laced themselves up into this constricting lingerie on a daily basis. (Indeed the fifties can be seen as an extraordinarily adventurous time for fashion, when women's breasts were thrust out like missiles, their feet brandished stilettos, which doubled as weapons of self-defence, and clothing not only followed the female form but actually reinvented it. Tina Turner and Madonna aside, who nowadays would have the nerve to look that blatantly sexual that much of the time?) The corset is a female armour that turns its wearer into a bodily hieroglyph of excessive femininity. Its opposite would be the healthy, desexualized nudity advocated by Scandinavian hygienists, or the white cotton underwear purchased for its natural qualities.

The boots, the corset. Aside from these key garments, the rest is variable – it could be leather, PVC, rubber – but in the sado-masochistic scenario of the popular imagination, the dominant cultural construction, the cruel woman is made to look intensely glamorous, she is the essence of libidinal voracity and power. Wanda, the original dominatrix, is an animal-lover's nightmare, her wardrobe overflowing with ermine, fox, sable and mink. And others of Sacher-Masoch's heroines, too, display their sexual power through the wearing of opulent clothing, velvet and satin, gold moire, and plenty of real jewellery.

Why are such images so popular? What is it that men seek from such fantasy figures? At first sight it seems clear that the dominatrix is the opposite side of the coin from the maternal aspect of femininity. No nurturing, no home-making is forth-coming from her, only the torturous discipline of the whip. Whatever she is, she certainly isn't mumsy. But more impor-tantly, perhaps, she is also not girlish. The Lolita-like appeal of wide-eyed schoolgirls, the look that Twiggy pioneered, now exemplified by Kate Moss, is way off the mark for the masochistic man. He needs not an innocent but a fully grown woman, and a bad one, like the female character Sada in Oshima's film *In the Realm of the Senses*, first encountered by her lover chasing another woman with a large kitchen knife. He suggests that she is so pretty that she should be holding something else, and this is a macabre hint of the way the film will end, with her holding a similar knife as she castrates him. Throughout the film, Sada behaves with spectacular nastiness, threatening to kill Kichi-san for sleeping with his wife, beating up one of the maids, forcing him to have sex with an elderly geisha. Each act of violence on her side is accompanied by increasing and palpable fascination on his, as his will gradually cedes completely to hers, to the point at which he surrenders his life to her.

The bad woman is essential. If she does not exist, she can always be invented, because someone is needed whom the male masochist can believe is bad or persuade to be bad. Per-haps he just wants to feel something strongly, anything, just to get the blood flowing through his veins. Perhaps the combat-ive woman figure is simply more sexual than her mild-man-nered sisters, there's a raw energy there that he wants to get in touch with. Perhaps he wants a woman to punish him for the sins of patriarchy, an erotic retribution. He could be in it for the challenge, the battle of wills. He is everyman, not some separate species.

But back to the S/M stage set that he has walked on to. We know how the cruel woman is dressed, but as for him, he may be dressed blandly, anonymously, unless he has a penchant for fancy dress: for instance, the slave outfit with a neck-ring attached to a leash that high-street sex shops will happily supply you with to enhance a dull winter evening.

Aside from costume, there is the question of setting. Imagine a boudoir resplendent with deep-red velvet drapes and sleazy satin sheets, low-level lighting, half-hidden pictures of Alpine landscapes and no windows: a claustrophobic environment. Or imagine a small room like the one in *In the Realm of the Senses*, hardly larger than the rumpled bed in its centre, in total disarray, reeking of delinquency, in which a series of pornographic Japanese woodcuts come to life in exquisite colour against a drab background of sliding screens.

The male masochist enters the world of narrative, of stories. The cultural form that embodies the possibility of things happening in time is literature, and particularly novels. Masochism did not begin with the novels of Sacher-Masoch; as I have tried to show, it is part of a long literary tradition. But the connection goes further than that.

A classic storyline, with roots in fairy-tale and folklore, is: boy meets girl, goes through some sort of trying ordeal to win her, finally succeeds and true love triumphs. There has to be some difficulty or resistance, a testing of the central character's mettle. This provides the tension for the reader, the sense of satisfaction when the hero comes up trumps. When the ordeal element is blown out of all proportion, you end up with a book describing the exploits of the SAS. When it is underplayed, a hospital romance.

The masochistic man opens himself up to the possibility of loss and gain through stepping out of his passive fascination with the image and into the world of narrative. He becomes, in a way, somehow human. This is because things are now required of him, he is going to have to play the game rather than stand to one side in the observer's box. Only by playing out the role does he discover and exploit his own resources, his capacity to flatter, cajole, persuade, impress, to elicit disgust, laughter or affection; in a word, to manipulate. He is impelled by longing, rather than acting consciously.

The odd thing about the masochistic narrative, which certainly follows the usual pattern of attraction, ordeal, erotic union, is that there is never a moment of triumph for the ego. In one sense the male masochist is skilful enough to accomplish a kind of erotic union that does not require him to act like a man. In this risqué relationship, the man hints at things that are generally concealed: his dislike of being male, and his wish to regain the irresponsibility of infancy, or to translate into a feminine register. It is only after his affair with Wanda is over that Severin is able to become a man, putting on his father's boots and becoming the master of the house; yet the ending strikes the reader as an intense disappointment. Perhaps manhood can be a let-down, and male masochism a paradoxical attempt to infuse more pleasure into it.

Due to men's traditional dignity in society, such role playing has to seem demeaning. Think of the gales of laughter that greet male students cross-dressing for rag week, or heterosexual men costumed as bunny girls for fancy-dress parties. It is easier for a woman to move up or down the scale, to be a childlike Marilyn or a masculinized 'tough cookie', without evoking the same uneasy ridicule.

This particular kind of sexual union can be used, in the case of the client, to avoid problems of commitment: the 'bad' woman is not to be loved. S/M is full of such reversals, which make it a useful excursion from everyday life. Yet masochistic fantasy can be pervasive, can encapsulate the meaning of desire itself.

In some senses sexual longing and identity seem to be opposed, as if being who you are (in my case, British, white, female, late thirties, a writer, etc.) is always an annoying suppression of all the other things you could be (too many possibilities to list). The only way of getting a life is to get lots of other people's, because they are *de facto* more interesting than your own. Sex is all about getting out of yourself and into someone else's skin, and the two best vehicles for accomplishing this are bodies and books.

An addiction to being sexually dominated is from this point of view an addiction to pure sex, an intensification of the usual thing, not something aberrant. One could deduce that the diminishing of the ego in masochism is a prelude to its annihilation during the sexual act. The masochist presents himself to his lover as risible in a process that will result in his temporary extinction, because that is the whole idea: to stop being oneself, to be invaded by the other person's presence.

There is nothing so unusual about wanting to leave one's identity behind. Any kind of real enjoyment enables a temporary forgetting of the self, whether it is gazing at a Giotto fresco or betting on the dogs. There is nothing so helpful and invigorating as excessive enjoyment. People who suffer from chronic, incurable pain find that although it cannot be stopped, any kind of enjoyment relieves it by enabling them to forget themselves for a while. But one doesn't have to be in pain to recognize the importance of self-forgetfulness. The reason that boredom is so miserable is because it means being continually conscious of oneself. The same applies to the jaded person who is unable to make use of the resources around them because a sense of surfeit allows no space inside, no hunger to draw in external stimuli.

If getting out of ourselves is what we are all doing (I am considering it as a positive aim, not something pathological), the male masochist has found what amounts to a cunning strategy of delivering himself up, pre-packaged, to sexual domination by a woman. Borrowing psychoanalytic terminology, I could say that it is as if the ego were laying itself open to being swallowed by the unconscious. Male masochists are subliminally aware of an irritation with their egos. (In fact we all are, but egos have made themselves indispensable, we cannot live without them.) Masochism dumps, indeed squashes the ego for a while in a pretty dramatic way.

Earlier I cited Sharon Stone's feminist challenge to the (especially male) viewer, a challenge that could be interpreted as, 'Occupy as many roles and sexual identities as I do.' But what I have been trying to show is that a large, indeed dominant, body of thought paralyses that possibility, nips it in the bud. The vocabulary of sexual normality freezes people into the adoption of single positions. That vocabulary, developed strongly by psychiatric discourses, has also been protected by psychoanalysis. Not for nothing does Freud smoke that enormous cigar, or sneer into the camera on the cover of the paperback copies of his work. No one has ever accused *him* of effeminacy.

Literature is the haven of fluidity, of slippage from one character to another, of movement. Women tend to read far more novels than men do, perhaps because this kind of ambiguous floating and flirtation is just what a self-protective masculinity needs to keep away from. Masculinity involves being faithful to oneself, high fidelity, singleness. But that allegiance to the truth of oneself can also lead to masochism, by a different route.

Infinitely Ravaged

Michel Leiris in *Manhood*, published in 1939 as *L'âge d'homme,* displays all the marks of over-defended masculinity that I have identified as this century's dubious heritage. But he works with and against them, even through a perceptible personal anguish, to enable masochistic wishes to emerge and encounters to happen. These are the central motifs of the book, a book which takes as its directing view the radical idea that sexuality is the cornerstone of the personality.

This autobiography presents itself as a simple confession, but one which uses a crucial motif to explain itself and build up its edifice. This is the painting by Lucas Cranach the Elder, *Lucretia and Judith*. In the Old Testament story, the widow Judith saves her city from invasion by the armies of the powerful general Holofernes by going to the enemy camp, becoming his concubine, and then beheading him while he sleeps. The hero of *Manhood*, Leiris tells us, is Holofernes, whose severed head Judith, on the right-hand side of the diptych, negligently dangles by its hair. Michel Leiris is identified with Holofernes, the man who is not only wounded but actually decapitated, who has lost not only his head but also control. Holofernes has become the sacrifice of Judith, a sacred, bloody trophy; he has been betrayed by bodily lust.

Leiris continually characterizes himself as wounded, vulnerable and erotically subjected. The crucial reference to the Cranach diptych allows him to explore this eroticism and project it upon the two figures in the painting. The story of the other woman in the painting, Lucretia, is a counterpoint to that of Judith. A virtuous wife whose fidelity makes her an object of lust for her husband's brother, Sextus Tarquin, Lucretia is raped by him, whereupon she commits suicide. In the picture she is shown pointing a dagger at her own heart, her eyes raised to heaven. The image encourages an enjoyment of aestheticized violation, and not for nothing: Leiris writes, 'Perhaps the only beautiful thing in life is to have been infinitely ravaged.'

The writing of this book grew out of the psychoanalytic treatment Leiris underwent for a year, after his own suicide attempt. Leiris really was a wounded man. So this is an attempt at writing a truthful book, one which tries to go beyond wish-fulfilment or formal beauty and instead to grasp something naked, a human reality of some sort.

He begins the novel by taking stock of himself in front of

the mirror, producing an inventory of defects and deformities. Yet he also tells the reader that whenever he catches sight of himself in the mirror, unprepared, he is utterly humiliated by the recognition of his own ugliness. It hardly needs saying that in fact Michel Leiris was rather good-looking, or at least photogenic. The point is that as a writer he starts his work by eliciting an unusual combination of ridicule and sympathy from the reader. He is also saying in a metaphorical way that the aesthetic of the book that is just beginning is not to do with classical, orchestrated elegance – which he considers anodyne and vain – but with the human pain, the confused, difficult eroticism, the damaged, ruined yet thriving emotions, the intensities and passions of everyday life. Whatever hurts, lives, and holds the only beauty that there is. The confession involves a personal exposure or even a (disgraceful) exhibition.

Manhood, in this book, is all about a life lived as close as possible to pain, erotic pain in particular. As the Lucretia and Judith painting indicates, the psychic and sexual confrontation with a woman is at the centre of Leiris's concerns. With this painting, it is as if the same woman (the two figures are identical) is put in two different positions. The adjacency of the two reinforces, for the author, the cruelty of the work, to the point where, he says, he feels faint in front of the painting. There's something powerful going on here. What is it that speaks to him so strongly? The Lucretia story certainly elucidates his own suppressed wishes, ones that are referred to explicitly.

'I sometimes saw my mother when she was getting ready for bed, and as much as I could, I used to watch her undress; I remember that one evening I hypocritically debauched myself while looking at her exposed bosom.' The mother is only in the next room, she seems accessible, but she is not. She belongs to the father, as Lucretia belongs to Tarquinius Collatinus. She can be secretly spied upon, but not touched with erotic intent. Is it the incest prohibition which confers upon his mother her desirability for the adolescent Michel, masturbating behind his bedroom door? Like Sextus Tarquin, he is denied access, but performs a kind of violation.

Leiris's pornographic homage to the figure of Lucretia is followed shortly afterwards by a gesture of dismissal of her servile devotion to conjugal morality, although actually it is her chastity which attracts the attentions of Sextus Tarquin. This contemptuous resentment precedes Leiris's extended meditation upon the figure of Judith and acts as one of the bridges between the two versions of femininity that exert such a strong influence on him.

In the diptych, Judith's veil and jewellery are more sumptuous than Lucretia's, her adornments more obvious. Lucretia rather ineffectually draws the fabric of her vestments about her. Her pose is that of a stricken martyr, with an expression of tragic anguish, her look is directed upwards. Judith looks relaxed and thoughtful, with a distant, perhaps melancholic look downwards. I imagine Judith as pitying Holofernes, while Lucretia evokes pity for herself. Despite her virtue, Lucretia displays herself fully to the gaze, while Judith appears to be walking away from the scene of the crime; there is a sense of movement and freedom. Judith, like Sacher-Masoch's Wanda, is a widow.

Cranach paints Judith and Lucretia after the act of making love with their enemies, Holofernes and Sextus Tarquin. The painting depicts the risk taken by both sexes on entering into a real encounter with the other.

If in the case of Lucretia the woman is the victim, in that of Judith it is the man who is put to death. Clearly the painting articulates Leiris's recurrent obsession with his own reception of pain. Chapters such as 'Cut throat', 'Inflamed genitals' and 'Hurt foot, bitten bottom, gashed head' describe various childhood accidents or illnesses. They follow directly after the chapter on Holofernes and unmistakably identify the narrator with the wounded man. The memories of being wounded are given an importance here which such minor incidents hardly seem to deserve. It is their aggregation which gathers significance around, for example, an operation in which the six-year-old Michel's tonsils are removed, or a minor inflammation of the penis.

Leiris sees himself as bound in advance for victimhood: already wounded (in extremely minor ways) during childhood, he wants nothing better than consciously to assume the same position as an adult male. For Leiris, Judith eclipses Lucretia, and if it is hard in life to find anyone who can fulfil the role, that does not prevent him from trying, via the 'crushed attitude' that he determinedly adopts.

The Judiths in his life appear in another inventory, like the list of childhood accidents. Many of the women he has never spoken to: Sarah Bernhardt and other inaccessible actresses, for example, or a young widow with bottle-blonde hair. These Judiths are equivalent to others, whores or mistresses, for whom the narrator's fascination has a deadly edge: an American woman who spoke of having committed a murder, a woman who showed a knife scar on her thigh. The list ends with a category of Judiths who are simply women with whom he dare not exchange a word, who render him speechless. Many of the women listed are cruel: others have cruelty thrust upon them. He seems to extract a wry pleasure from the confessions of being bitten, kicked in the face, of falling into impotence, being ridiculed and humiliated by these Judiths. The latter form a category of women 'who attract me to the same extent that they escape me or paralyse and terrify me'.

In the original Old Testament story, Judith outwits death by her trickery and artifice. To that extent she is exemplary for the project of Leiris himself, on the one hand pleading pathetically for sympathy from the reader, on the other serving up a heady cocktail of exhibitionism, auto-eroticism, incest, sadism and masochism, and getting away with it by making it art. With Judith, he passes from an unhappy, tortured identification with a woman to a powerful one. When a woman is dominant, it creates a particular kind of male identification, an identification with power, which makes a temporary giving-up of the masculine position a little easier.

This temporary, imaginative sex change parallels an episode in the autobiography in which he meets the first love of his life, Kay. He has not yet become her lover, and the two of them, with another couple, decide to dress up. Kay dresses as a man. Michel puts on a dress and she helps him to put on make-up. 'All difficulty was removed for me, since, thanks to my transvestism, I only had to let myself go.'

Kay feminizes his name to Micheline, the name his mother would have called him if he had been born a girl. Only by renouncing his manhood, becoming Micheline, can he become Kay's lover, thereby in reality assuming it. It is as if their exchange of clothing – Kay borrows his hat, cane and suit – opens up a possibility for another kind of exchange: a dialogue between the sexes.

Or perhaps just a temporary truce in the sex war. Jesuit works on rhetoric from the period of the Counter-Reformation represent Judith as an ascetic adapting herself to the role of courtesan to trick and destroy her adversary. Judith was a symbol of eloquence, in particular the triumphant eloquence of the Church. In such discourses, Judith is invested with a potential for speech which is used in a similar way to her feminine artifices: to destroy, outwit, overwhelm, ruin the speech of the other. This view of Judith links her to Sacher-Masoch's heroines, who combine intellectual and sexual power, definite world views with plunging necklines and pearls. Boys will be girls and girls will be boys, as the words from the musical *Cabaret* have it. But boys actually want to be a particular kind of girl, the clever, entrepreneurial, amusing girl – Fanny Ardant

in François Truffaut's film *Vivement Dimanche*, for example –
not some wilting violet.

The dominatrix refuses to be repressed by masculine domination, has her own analysis, her own distinct aims, her own
ruthless strategies of seduction and betrayal. The order that is
disrupted by her challenge is what Michel Leiris calls 'the ferocious order of virility'. Holofernes' head, severed from its
body, and upon which Leiris does not comment, is not that of
a repulsive monster, but that of a handsome, rather ascetic
man. His expression is one of anguished abandonment. But
Holofernes is dead.

In the stories of both women in the Cranach diptych, somebody ends up dead. While his cross-dressing with Kay opens
up the utopian potential for a dialogue, what Leiris actually
presents is a duel, a bullfight, in which one or other of the protagonists must be annihilated by the other. An unending conflict is the human reality, conflict internal and external. This
war is the raw stuff of a life that burns, and burns out.

Yet masculine masochism is more of a calculated risk than
this autobiography implies. The traversal of a terrain of violence is only begun in the longing for erotic union, and the risk
involved guarantees a full sexual charge to the encounter.
Nothing guarantees an upsurge so much as a preliminary
defeat. This is what the male masochist knows, and the reason
he is such a consummate strategist, a better one than
Holofernes.

5 Reckonings

Perversity

Some kinds of knowledge come from outside, from spaces of exile. Sometimes thoughts seem to come from somewhere that consciousness would like to disown, they don't always present themselves as being useful to the daily projects of survival, acceptance, fulfilment, so you deflect them and get on with whatever you are *meant* to be doing: typing, ironing.

If you could store this waste matter over a period of time, instead of discarding it, it would probably reflect an interestingly variegated picture of other ways of conceiving yourself, not just in terms of ready-made, finished versions, but the half-glimpsed fragments of how things could be or might have been for you, images that touch you briefly and find a response, like a dull note on the piano or the harsh pitch of a bird call. You imagine what it would have been like if you had been a man rather than a woman, you suddenly see yourself as you will look in twenty years' time, or as you were at fourteen. There are many other places and times to inhabit, some pure fiction, others with a basis in your own existence.

If you could then make this fabric communicable you would end up with something called culture – films, novels, plays, which give you a safe place in which to imagine living and dying differently from the way you are doing. And actually everybody has their own personal culture, their repertoire of the images that touch them, their flashes of unexpected identification, their repressed wish to be somebody else. It is just that we do not tend to take these things particularly seriously, we do not appreciate these moments.

To recognize such moments is to recognize oneself – suddenly and distortedly perhaps – in a different mirror, a mirror that discloses the hidden longings, defects, disappointments, aberrations. It is not immodest or pretentious to develop an individual and intuitive place in the world, it is a kind of craft of tangential self-knowledge, it's about learning to recognize yourself in unexpected places. Michel Leiris began to formulate a project of the kind, which he called the sacred in everyday life, looking upon the symbols of the kitchen stove, his father's top hat and wallet, and other ordinary artefacts as imbued with a mythical importance.

It is not just familiar objects, familial contexts that are significant, though this is a step in that direction. Truman Capote said of Andy Warhol that he would have liked to be anybody other than the person he actually was. Although this was meant to signify his pathos, perhaps this was Warhol's gift, his sense that everyone had something about them worthy of interest, if only for five minutes. There is nothing stimulating or exciting about being yourself, except when you see yourself anew through the eyes of somebody else, and that isn't often a particularly flattering experience.

There is a central self that I know reasonably well, because the external factors of our lives hold it in place: for example, I live in a flat in London with my boyfriend, I start the day with a strong coffee, then move on to work at the computer, I visit the library and often meet friends. This fabric holds my life loosely together, gives it a perceptible shape.

But sometimes I think that things may turn out quite differently from the way I now conceive them. Sometimes one leaves behind probability and assumption, one moves into the world of *what if*? How far should we follow up the sometimes fragmentary, sometimes insistent images that present themselves, from nowhere? One view is that you should go for it, and live out your fantasies. For those of us who, with some

justice, could be accused of being fantasists, this is impractica-
ble. We would need many hundreds of lives to fulfil the
dreams of a single one.

Other views promote the resolutely singular, and such people are strongly observant of what is in front of them. I am not
particularly admiring of this, since such people lose out on the
pleasure of leaving the self behind and finding it again, indefin-
ably different. Even something that seems as banal as buying a
new pair of shoes can become an adventure, with each pose in
front of the angled mirror revealing a different way of imagining oneself. That is why the question of a personal image is not
trivial, and changing your image is a valid imaginative act.
Readers may be able to call up moments when, for example,
taking a bag of tired garments to the charity shop or investing
in an Armani silk dress seemed like a turning point in their
lives, a gateway to a new vision of the possible.

All these fragmented day-dreams, these narcissistic flights
of fancy, might be termed perverse, with an overtone of disapproval. What could be more perverse than, for example, imagining that you are a member of the opposite sex (and perhaps
dressing up in their clothes, transvestism), or finding yourself
subliminally or explicitly attracted by someone of your own
sex? The intensity of such moments is due in part to their
transgressive quality, their going against one's central, seemingly necessary self.

Once such possibilities are legitimated, turned into singular,
concrete entities, rather than played with or flirted with, they
begin to lose this quality. A militant gay scene may scorn heterosexuals for a presumed conventionality and conservatism,
denying its own internal pluralism. And there are people who
defend their right surgically to change sex. The very univocal
way in which they proclaim their subsequent contentment
makes me intensely suspicious. If you have longed for something, and got it, you do not easily excise longing from your

emotional make-up. It just goes somewhere else. Perversity, considered in a non-judgemental way, is about keeping things moving rather than tying them down.

Critical theorist Jonathan Dollimore argues that homosexuality is transgressive in its challenge of the dominant heterosexual order, he sees it as a container of the perverse impulse, which can never be brought under control. This is an interesting idea on the political level, proposing a view of an oppressive system that insists strongly on its own singularity, its own truth to itself, its exclusivity. If this were so, it would suggest a terrible structural weakness in the social order, since the more that perversity is denied, the more disgraceful tends to be its eventual eruption. I am not sure that this culture is as fragile as that. What Dollimore is critiquing is a conservative high moral ground that is practically extinct outside religious circles, except for the purposes of occasional political rhetoric. And lesbians and gay men are not the only perverse people around, though it is certainly they who have brought questions of sexual diversity to the forefront of contemporary thought.

Perversity or perversion – there is quite a difference between these two words. 'Perversion' is a clinical term, that has been used to cover the child-molester in the same breath as the masochist or the invert (homosexual). 'Perversity' is a term which denotes not sexuality, but a tendency to err from the straight and narrow, to depart from the true path. What perversity and perversion have in common is simply a decision to differ from the prescribed way of behaving. Yet in the *Concise Oxford Dictionary*, one definition given under the word 'perverse' is 'wicked'. Both perversity and perversion still suffer from this kind of demonization, as if they were a kind of witchcraft whose practitioners should be burnt. And the dangerous, risky aura of the perverse is also an important element in its attraction.

So transgression can take place on two levels. First by the

entertaining of a fantasy life and its translation into actual experience, something that may be described more obviously as 'succumbing to desire', a falling down or away from loyalty to a singular, perhaps sexually unsatisfying existence. Such excursions into erotic landscapes could happen in diverse ways, and the individual feels somehow restored by the experience though they may not have much of an inkling why they should be. The one-night stand, the office affair after hours, are only the most obvious examples of ways that people fulfil the aching need for perverse transgression. Other less direct means include conversion to evangelical Christian worship, spending over the limit of your bank account, having your nipples pierced, dangerous sports, indulgence in cream cakes, and marrying somebody that your family doesn't approve of. The list could run and run. It includes almost everybody. The common factor is the negation of an ideal. Cream cakes are 'naughty but nice' as they used to be advertised, because they ruin your attempts at staying slim, keeping an ideal body. Diving off one of the towers of Battersea Power Station with a piece of elastic tied to one ankle is a more visceral challenge, directed against ideals of prudency.

A stronger, more confident level of transgression goes further. While the first category seeks camouflage and has ready excuses for misbehaviour, the second is populated by truly wayward people, who want their perversities noticed. The perversities in the first category can eventually be recouped and legitimated: the office affair ends by becoming a live-in relationship, nipple-piercing becomes fashionable rather than subcultural. The second group resists such reintegration within the norm, knowing that the pleasure of their perversity or perversion depends on maintaining a taunting, subversive distance. Many marijuana smokers don't want to see this soft drug legalized because the whole culture that they belong to would be rendered toothless at one fell swoop. And many gay men do not want to see homosexual culture embraced by straight people and given a place in the sun, for similar reasons: they would lose their edge, their challenging difference from the ordinary man in the street, their distinctive presence.

Masochism comes into both categories, in that it is practised both covertly and overtly. The title of this book implies that I would like to see it brought in out of the cold, redescribed as just part of many people's sexual make-up and activity, an acceptable form of kinkiness. That is not quite on target. In fact I am arguing for the breaking-down of notions of normality, a coexistence of disparate ways of occupying one's skin, one's eroticism. That would involve a relaxation of the tension around perverse transgression, a tension that it is in many people's perceived interests to maintain.

One reason that this proposal would offend would be for the reasons I have already mentioned: people who now enjoy sado-masochistic practices might feel that they would lose the desirable sense of offending public decency, or being a member of a subculture with all the special knowledge and history that entails. (That is setting aside the more obvious opposition of the moral-majority kind.) Rebels want to stay rebels, they thrive in this role. This isn't to trivialize the role of the rebel, just to argue that the cause may be more contingent than crucial. (Thriving societies value dissidents – and put them to work – for their infusion of vital tensions into the social fabric.)

That is not the same as saying that every kind of transgressive sexual practice is identical to another. If homosexuality aims to outrage orthodoxy, what would happen if through cultural acceptance it lost all its shock value, as is beginning to happen? Gay men could not easily maintain their edge by just switching to some other form of perversion. It is only the shoes that pinch that one throws off. Only the ideals that suffocate or squash one's vitality are targeted by perverse actions or identifications.

Such ideals are usually linked in some way with a censoring, parental figure. In the imagination, the lesbian or masochist or transvestite is continually outraging that person by offending an ideal that they embody. Are sexual dissidents, then, just permanent adolescents, people who are so stuck in difficult love–hate affairs with parental figures that all they can ever do is continually re-enact them through making aberrant choices of partners or behaving scandalously? And not only that, but making sure that everybody knows about it? It does seem likely that there's an element of this in what we call perversion, but that doesn't undermine it or qualify its value. To carry around the spark generated by a relationship with a parent probably means that as an adult you can deploy levels of sexual and creative energies denied to more well-behaved, less well-invested others. The resentment that characterizes the period of transition from childhood to adulthood is accompanied by a growing freedom, and a sense of experimentation. These qualities are permanently preserved by people who are sexually perverse. Any reduction in public censoriousness towards perversity and perversion would tend to show more clearly that such matters are, in their essence, entirely private. It would deflate the fantasy of social censorship acting as the negative guarantor of sexual transgression.

My view is that whatever happens, fantasy will not go away. The desire to find out, human curiosity at the most basic level, is inexhaustible. Perversions and perversities are not exchangeable, but they are capable of development, elaboration. To be thoroughly perverse is actually quite difficult. It involves being in touch with one's most fleeting, insubstantial, nebulous, inconstant wishes, being spontaneous (and daring) enough to act on them (or merely enjoy them passing) and relaxed enough not to tie them down too much. It is, in fact, an art.

Masochism has a perverse content to it in that it transgresses ideals of self-affirmation, courage, bodily integrity. The opposing figure to the masochist is the fearless hero or woman war-rior. In their everyday life people who enjoy sexual masochism are likely to be the assertive, risk-taking kind, living up to the ideal that is deflated and turned inside out in the bedroom. (This is because sex has something of a balancing function, sneaking back into your life the sordid elements that you have attempted to get rid of in your conscious dealings.) They are anything but the 'moral masochists' on whom Freud poured scorn. The ruthless politician who loses his seat in the Com-mons may go off his usual sexual fare of being treated like a child or tortured. The more successful you are in your daily life, the more fascinating masochism may start to seem. And at the other end of the spectrum, the rapist can be clearly seen as somebody so weak and pathetic that he has to compensate by forcing himself on someone who doesn't find him attractive.

Masochism also goes beyond the perverse, in that it is uni-versal, deeply embedded as an imaginative possibility, and is an intrinsic and wide-ranging aspect of cultural life. This is something that has suffered from lasting misrecognition. Indeed, misunderstanding has been masochism's fortune in all sorts of ways.

Sheffield

It is 1990. A circle of gay men in Sheffield get together for the purpose of S/M sex. Their activities involve hitting the penis with a ruler, caning and dripping hot wax on the genitals. Somebody has the idea of putting some of their scenes on video, the tapes pass into police hands, and Operation Spanner is born. As in some television cop series, they swoop, make mass arrests, and *although everybody concerned is a consent-ing adult*, fifteen get sentences, five of these prison sentences. Dangerous games.

In Britain, the law is showing itself less and less willing to prosecute sado-masochists. In 1996 an S/M night-club owner, charged with running a disorderly house, was released, not guilty, in spite of the fact that he was allowing a room at the club to be used for his customers' sexual encounters. A survey of the public by the Law Commission, the government's legal adviser, showed that most people are unsympathetic to the prosecution of those who indulge in sado-masochism and consider it a matter for the individual. This resulted in the Commission's recommendation that consenting adults should be immune from prosecution for sado-masochistic sex. But in early 1997 that liberalising movement was thrown on to the defensive with the European Court's upholding of the convictions in the Spanner case, on the basis that assault cannot be consented to.

Yet people can consent to far more physically damaging practices without falling foul of the law: for example, being beaten unconscious in a public boxing match, with the concomitant probability of life-long brain damage; or undergoing a sex-change operation that involves permanent surgical removal of the penis and testicles, or breasts in the case of women, with reconstruction of secondary body parts. Nor are there any special medical or ethical grounds for such practices being given preferential treatment by the law over masochistic consensual practices.

There is something interesting about the meeting of the two worlds, so similar in their concern with the meting-out of punishment. In the world of the sado-masochist, handcuffs and chains are just as important as in the world of the police officer. The uniformed fascist has an important role to play in gay and masochistic iconography. It is a comic cliché that not just a certain kind of woman but also some gay men are supposed to adore soldiers and policemen, who respond with predictable unease. Masochists amuse themselves and take pleasure in playing the persecuted, crushed victim, and sado-masochism could be seen as a kind of extended joke about law and order, or if not exactly a joke, certainly a parodic invocation of it for erotic purposes. Taken out of context, the notion of 'law and order' can be sexualized or, more accurately, can show itself to be, at base, another kind of sexual fantasy. Masochists are sophisticated mockers of a rageful conventionality, which revenges itself by enacting its own unselfconscious desire to put the boot in.

Criminals activate the law and keep it in operation; criminality keeps the system of punishment going and the prisons overflowing. In some senses all criminals must know how central, how meaningful they are to the criminal-justice system. Of course, this is stretching a point, but one could even argue that they are its authors, the policemen mere agents of their need to be brought to book occasionally. In this sense the criminal covertly engineers his or her own culpability and conviction in a way that echoes with the masochist's initiation of the sado-masochistic contract. But the two worlds – that of sado-masochistic, parodic sex, and that of crime and punishment – should never be confused. While the policeman is the criminal's opposite number, the voluntary torturer is the masochist's.

The European Court's decision on the Spanner case has troubling implications for the sex lives of everyone. We will not, hopefully, be seeing policemen tumble into our bedrooms, but we are being legally discouraged from exploring an aspect of our sexuality that is universal, valuable and exciting. Responsibility for our own actions is being removed and assumed by the state, in an invasion of personal rights.

This backlash against sexual freedom is the same kind that first brought masochism into disrepute over a century ago. From being an illness, it is now definable as a crime. A century's misunderstandings have contributed to that criminalization.

Coupling

The idea that sex should be gentle, loving and caring is not only generally approved but even generally prescribed. Other approaches to the sexual act tend to be treated with suspicion or ridicule, or can even set off paranoid reactions. For example, consensual sado-masochism can be believed to lead to actual bodily harm by some ineluctable, irresistible downward path. Yet there is no evidence for this.

Such widespread anxieties are hard to explain. One argument that has been put forward in response to mainstream paranoia is that it bears witness to the persecutory nature of the social order. Society is seen from this perspective as bent on securing and displaying its own continuing power by forcing all members of society to follow rigid patterns of sexual behaviour, and making scapegoats of any dissidents.

I feel this is too monolithic a view of a society that is in fact heterogeneous rather than uniform, that is capable of some level of evolution and has gradually become more relaxed on questions of sexuality, though strait-laced attitudes are still prevalent. All I can offer is the view that sex can be such a strong experience that it may seem to need taming so as not to overwhelm. The shattering quality of sex needs to be diluted for those who cannot fully handle it, and it does seem that these people still vastly outnumber those who *can* handle a wide-ranging field of erotic experience. The former category make a kind of civic virtue from their own necessity to retreat from the challenge of a full-blooded encounter, and protect themselves via a battery of psychological defences.

There are all sorts of worrying echoes in this restricted view of what sex should and should not involve. A narrowness of outlook persists. My early conception of sex was of a man lying on top of a woman, penetrating her. This raw, simplified image, like an obscene scrawl on the wall of a men's toilet, seemed to be the only way that sex was represented or thought of then: it was the prescribed position. Sex was something offensive and sordid that men did to women and women tried their hardest to avoid. Other comparable views, at best termed Victorian, at worst inhuman, are still around – for example, many people still condemn as 'promiscuous' women who have had more than one lover. And the view that only sick people prefer members of their own sex has not quite disappeared – though like these other soul-destroying attitudes, it is on the way out.

There is no obvious reason why sex should always be loving and gentle, any more than why it should be done in the same position, with somebody of the opposite sex, or be restricted to the bedroom. In fact, the less variety sex includes, the less it is likely to involve or arouse the people taking part. Bland sexuality is no sexuality at all.

As I have remarked before, there is a distinct divergence between the demands of what we might call pure love, and those of eroticism. Love does not ask for excitement, but sexuality depends on it. Love involves a hospitality towards another person, it means bringing them within your own boundaries; sexual desire demands that these boundaries be broken down. It is the sense of drama and reversal, of the enacting of a narrative with a beginning, a middle and an end, that gives sex its particular quality. But love does not have a story; it is what happens when we reach the end of the story, epitomized by the words 'happily ever after'. For the erotic, this phrase is the knell of doom, signalling the end of all arousing tension.

The tension between the two groups of demands is not easily resolved – and this is what many couples discover, to their chagrin. In the early period of the relationship, both are met. Since the other person has not yet been taken into oneself, through the extension of love, they remain other enough to satisfy the erotic need for a real sense of contact. But once the period of mutual discovery and exploration is over, the sexual tension becomes eroded. The two individuals in the couple become more like one person, the boundaries between them dissolved, and for all the right reasons: love, trust, mutual co-operation. This is still likely to happen even if they make a decision to maintain separate interests and friendships, and the persistence of sexual boredom is likely to lead to one member starting an affair. Yet the memory of the early days is still clear, tauntingly so in that the unique combination of circumstances then present can never recur. The phenomenon of serial monogamy bears witness to the enduring hope that such circumstances can be recreated, the enduring wish to have one's cake and keep on eating it.

One alternative to sexual betrayal – doing the same dance all over again with another person – is sexual experimentation, or trying out some new ideas with the same person. In sado-masochistic sex, the division of roles between the dominant partner and the submissive partner ensures that a boundary is maintained, since each is required to act differently. The need to play out the role also places the participant under pressure, especially if this is not the couple's usual kind of sexual engagement. Both partners have to hone their acting skills, at the very least.

What is actually involved, apart from the desire of both partners to try something new, that allows different kinds of longings and satisfactions to emerge, that potentially reveals new facets of the other person and of oneself, and that allows each person to view the other in a new way? The decision even to consider confessing one's fantasies is already a big step, and requires a lot of trust. For example, because of the contempt that masochism can evoke, it may be difficult for a person who is extroverted and bossy in their usual persona to admit that they like nothing better than to be tied to the bed and forced into sexual submission.

It is hard to overcome, between two people, the kind of sneering, prurient attitude towards sexual variation that pervades this culture, and simultaneously to throw off the everyday personality armour that you may need to get through the day. Nobody is really a singular, solid entity, absolutely the same in every context, and as I have already tried to show, it is particularly in the erotic context that these kinds of role reversals should be expected. Desire is all about what you have not got, what you have not already made your own, all about turning the everyday scheme of things inside out. This first step involves the admission of a fully-functioning fantasy life, the admission of wishes that are incompatible with one's ideals, even opposed to them. And this may only be made with someone you can trust, for example, a partner with whom you have developed a caring relationship.

While the straight couple is well placed for these kinds of explorations, there are other couplings in which they also thrive. I am thinking in particular of lesbians and gay men, people who are already sexual outlaws or dissidents. Sadomasochism has been an important part of gay sexuality for a long time, and has been put forward as a kind of extreme form of sexual revolt by writers like Pat Califia and Edmund White. Within these subcultures, already defined by particular sexual desires, there seems to be a more developed comprehension and integration of alternative eroticisms. The movement out of the circle of heterosexual exchange has opened up space for further experimentation.

Gay men and lesbians frequently have shaven heads and wear tough, skinhead-type clothing, for sexual as well as confrontational reasons. This dress style signifies a strong, confident presence, it invokes the violence that has been directed at sexual dissidents, turning it back on the onlooker, and it is a statement about physicality. It presents a sexuality that is aggressive and uncompromising rather than soft, sensual, inviting. Within gay culture, there is an immediacy about the issue of sex itself; it is higher up on the agenda than in straight culture. There used to be an argument which would apologize defensively for homosexuality, on the grounds that gay couples living together could be as monogamous and otherwise conformist as any heterosexual married couple. Nowadays, the boot seems to be gradually being laced on to the other foot, with heterosexuals ruefully coming to recognize that gay men and lesbians often have better sex lives than they do.

Whether we are talking about a gay or straight couple, an openness about one's fantasies and longings is a prerequisite for any sado-masochistic encounter. Such a couple might negotiate a deal, by which each listens to the other's ideas and agrees to help act them out. Of course there might be numerous fantasies other than masochistic ones – some which might have to remain restricted to fantasy because of being too ambitious, unethical or repellent to the other partner to be acted out. Unless a fantasy scenario has some appeal for both partners, it is unlikely to find its way into their sexual repertoire. However, one person is often attracted to another because of an intuitive sense that this particular person can relate to their fantasy life. This is a delicate matter, though, and the worst outcome might be for one of the partners continually to push for their own favourite sexual experiment, with the other feeling pressured into going along with it. Sado-masochism does offer a satisfying role for both people, though perhaps more so for the masochist who generally initiates it and attempts to makes it attractive to the other partner. As your life changes, so do your sexual interests and desires, and masochism may be a single experiment or a long-term preference.

The lack of sensitive, accessible discussion of sexual issues (as opposed to 'good sex' videos, exploitative pornography or well-meaning but specialist scholarly works) leaves, I imagine, most people in the dark as to how to deal with their own desires. At least, this is the case as soon as those desires are understood to be out of the norm, in some way apart from the restricted eroticism that is everywhere advocated. For this reason, I make no apology for the agony-aunt suggestion that both members of any couple should be able to articulate their wishes and have them considered. This would counter the danger of one member ending up as the pawn of the other's desires. However nice it would be, nobody can expect their partner to identify fully with their own fantasy. Rather, it should be understood that each partner has the chance to direct a particular scene, and certainly to bow out if left cold by the other's ideas. It is, of course, possible for both members to come towards the same idea from their own imaginations, resulting in a perfectly complementary sexual narrative. But this is analogous to both members reaching a climax at the same time – desirable, yet unlikely.

Having made the decision to exchange confidences, and to enact one or two chosen fantasies that are interesting to both partners, how would things proceed? I have already discussed the importance of particular kinds of costume, of an iconography, a setting and a story, a narrative development. There is also the question of a contract. The contract has always been an important element in the masochistic relationship.

This is because masochism, as a human tendency, is not generally taken for granted, or even understood. It has to seek agreement and consent in a special way, to clear a space for itself and to specify its own boundaries. Because any form of masochistic sex is challenging, by its nature it is open to misinterpretation, and as I have pointed out, paranoid misinterpretation at that. The contract between the couple is an attempt to prevent things going wrong in a climate adverse to such explorations. It also enshrines the principle of agreement, like a subversive, temporary marriage contract. After all, marriage is only a more socially acceptable kind of deal between two people.

A sexual contract can also be a lot of fun for anyone who has ever made one. Severin stipulated that Wanda should wear furs as often as possible in return for his acting as her servant. The contract can include all sorts of comical quasi-legal clauses and sub-clauses, with a tongue-in-cheek solemnity. It can involve the assuming of alternative names and identities, prescribe certain forms of behaviour and proscribe others, elaborate an etiquette between the two partners, specify the duration of the masochistic set-up and its exact location. It celebrates a collusion between the two partners, a decision to stick to a role and thoroughly act it out, even in front of anonymous others.

A contract does not have to be written down, although that is an interesting and amusing possibility, and there can be many kinds of contracts, each one succeeding the last. It can happen through mutual understanding or through verbal agreement. But some kind of contract is essential. From that, the couple moves to the core of the action.

Whiplash

The action is mainly the preserve of the dominant partner. Masochism involves passivity, the masochist is the one who undergoes the treatment. That does not mean that he or she has no part to play, rather that the part consists mainly in the adoption of specific poses. There is a repertoire of classic masochistic gestures, which includes the bowed head, bended knee, lowered eyes, hands that supplicate or serve.

A woman cited in a Jungian study found that she enjoyed serving her lover with a glass of wine as he reposed arrogantly, ordering her around, being waited on. This would be a typical opening gambit, the setting-up of contrasting bodily postures that signify master and slave positions. The masochistic pose is one of exaggerated servility, the body language speaks of weakness and even shame. It shows that the individual has abnegated his own will and is ready to be imprinted by the will of the dominant partner, he puts himself at her disposal.

The torturer, too, takes up positions that clearly mark dominance: she may stand towering above the passive partner (which is part of the reason for the impossibly high heels), or she may raise her hand in a threatening gesture or frown like an offended tsarina.

These postures recur throughout the masochistic encounter, and may give it an odd temporal quality; while quiet, caring sex is at its best caressing and smooth flowing, sado-masochism seems to pause as each partner assumes the next pose and then start off again with some swift movement. With each pause, each successive, formalized act, the story unfolds, each stage building tension up to saturation point before moving on to the next.

Early on there is likely to be a staging of undressing, with the submissive partner either stripping or being stripped. This isn't the clumsy button-popping tearing-off of the outer garments that precedes simple, carnal copulation. It may become a ritual involving bathing, for example, where the whole body, including skin and hair, is groomed for the encounter to come. The submissive partner leaves their previous persona behind them in the bath water, emerging purified of their own ego and ready to accept the imposition of the dominant partner's will. This stripping and bathing represents an interim stage between the initial appearance of the submissive partner and his full entry into the masochistic exchange, a stage at which he has been deprived of his own identity but is not yet physically invaded by the other person. As I have previously indicated, where there is masochism, there is always a concern with dirt – getting rid of it is only a prerequisite for really getting down into it.

Either naked or possibly robed in some form of slave outfit, he now may be blindfolded and tied to a pillar (despite the dearth of pillars in contemporary architecture, they regularly crop up in masochistic literature) and then made to wait while the torturer prepares herself for the infliction of cruelty. Waiting is another form of forced passivity, producing the sense of being a target for the capricious, unpredictable lusts of the other partner, and bondage is one of the crucial elements of masochism. The leather strips or nylon cords used rub and bite into the skin, beginning the build-up of a confused but intense physical response. The restraint that they enforce denies any outward expression of longing and therefore intensifies it internally in the person who cannot move his limbs, who is pinioned to a bedpost. In masochistic pornography the submissive partner is often gagged and blindfolded to increase the sense of being absolutely unable to control the situation. When every means to act has been eliminated, the willing victim is completely focused upon what is happening to him, what he feels, his sensory responses. Not surprisingly, they are extremely heightened by his situation.

The torturer stands in front of the victim. The victim may be blindfolded or his sight may be partially obscured, if he has been tied up in a particular position. His vision, and all his sensory impressions are fragmented, made partial by his own tension and feverish response. He may see only a pair of high-heeled leather boots and the hand clutching a whip. He may hear only a sardonic laugh and the cords of the whip trailing lightly along the floor. This anticipatory purgatory is an important part of the game, the turning of the screw to the point at which the victim longs for the pain to happen now, to end the agony of waiting. The masochist who initiated this programme feels faint-hearted, now the game has taken over and he has lost control.

The reader may wonder at this point if things really have got out of control. There does need to be some possibility for the passive partner to get out of the situation if he begins to feel that he cannot handle it. Yet because of the ironic reversals involved in sado-masochistic sex, every 'no' may mean 'yes'. Sado-masochistic sex involves a linguistic invalidation of the negative. And this is another reason why masochistic encounters work best between people who know they can trust each other. The couple needs to agree in advance on a word or gesture that really does mean 'no', and that can be deployed by the masochist if he feels things have gone too far. But one of the crucial skills of the dominant partner is to make sure that does not happen. It is a difficult task to get sexual dominance right – go too far and your partner feels devastated, not far enough and they feel short-changed. Domination is less popular than is generally imagined – it carries too many responsibilities.

After what seems an endless suspension of time, the whip comes down. The whip is the preferred instrument of masochism. This sexual violence is carefully controlled and orchestrated, and bodily contact is minimal. The immediate sharp, extreme pain makes the passive partner forget all about the waiting that seemed so unbearable a moment ago. This pain goes right through him and cuts out consciousness of anything else. The whip may come down on back, bottom or thighs; every lash leaves a mark behind and makes the victim squirm with pain.

In itself this whipping is anything but pleasurable. It is only a prerequisite for the sexual contact that is expected afterwards. The flaying-away of all psychological tension forces the participant to inhabit their body fully, as a receptive, passionate vessel, leaving a fresh, clear space. Having taken this punishment, the body is alive to sensation, fully aroused to its own receptiveness and longing for positive sensuality. At this point both people are ready to release themselves into sexual pleasure and satisfaction.

Of course, masochistic sex can take a number of different avenues; the one I have described here is just what I consider the most classic form. Sexual surrender is anything but formulaic. If it becomes so, it is likely to result in boredom. And that would be a pity.

6 The Uses and Abuses of Suffering

The Body of Christ

Previous chapters in this book have been devoted to exploring the various aspects of masochistic experience, its historical construction, its differing nature for men and women, its relation to the image, to literature and so on. I have tried to stay close to the question of the erotic in all these aspects, to the particular attraction of masochistic love and the emotional and identificatory needs it tends to serve.

In this final chapter, I want to go a little further than that, to speculate about masochism as a force in cultural life, to try to locate the ways in which it is present beyond the immediately sexual and beyond questions of gender. The crucial question here is of the universal kind, the kind that can never be answered satisfactorily, but that demands a provisional response at the very least. It can be framed most simply as, 'What is the best way to handle suffering?' One of the reasons why this question is important is because we now realize that advances in technology have not delivered what was once signalled as their aim – the abolition of suffering. The political scene has also shown itself unable to alleviate suffering, though the promise to do so is at the centre of all political agendas. The futuristic desire that people have harboured over the course of the century, for a body without internal organs, covered with armour plate and without subjectivity – the robot – is only a fantasy, and may be more of a nightmare. What is clear is that we have thin skins, we bleed when pricked, we catch diseases that science cannot cure; in a thousand ways, we suffer.

Suffering cannot be prevented; as a general category, there is a kind of absolute limit to any kind of therapeutic discourse. There is no cure for death, neither is there any for all the signs of mortality that accompany you or me right through the duration of our lives. Such signs tend to appear on and in the body, because bodies are always imperfect, with teeth that decay, eyes that need glasses, bad backs, sore skin or worse. Of course, dentists, opticians, physiotherapists and dermatologists are necessary, but they can only perform a limited function. The role of medical practitioners has become inflated by the wishful thinking that they can resolve pain, disease, even madness.

The brutal truth is that human beings are perishable. When religion was an active force, belief in the immortality of the soul meant that the mortality of the body was a considerably less disagreeable fact than it is today. Now mass credulity is invested in the notion of the cure for the body's ills, since the life of the body is considered to be all there is.

How does masochism relate to the question of suffering? In one way that is immediately obvious: where the general tendency is to do everything to avoid pain, in masochism it is invited into the centre of the scene. There is a seeming reversal of meanings, which is why masochism has often been termed 'paradoxical'; instead of pain signifying horror, it represents the gateway to erotic satisfaction. Those who have never understood the attraction of masochism must wonder how it is that masochists can turn something so undesirable into the very fabric of their satisfaction. They find it hard to comprehend the complex psychosexual manoeuvre that masochists perform, the virtuosity with which they exploit their secret knowledge, which is that at the kernel of mortality lies the most intense erotic charge.

Etsuko, the passionate heroine of Yukio Mishima's novel *Thirst for Love*, understands this connection and tries to take control of her life through this insight. As her philandering husband Ryosuke lies dying of typhoid fever, she feels happy for the first time since the beginning of her marriage. 'How alike they were – her honeymoon and her husband's death – two short periods of joy! Now she travelled with him to death's resort. There was on this trip, as on the wedding journey, the same abuse of body and soul, the same untiring, insatiable desire and pain.'

Some months after Ryosuke's death, Etsuko falls in love. Once more the eroticism that floods through her body is exquisitely deadly, with suicide imagined as a kind of sensual release. '. . . she suddenly thought of poisoning herself. As she imagined the joy of feeling the white crystals of the poison spread in the water and quietly penetrate her bloodstream, Etsuko fell into a kind of rapture and shed tears that caused her not the slightest pain.'

People who invite pain represent themselves as sufferers – both to themselves and to those others who deal out the punishment. Masochists wallow in their pain, let it take over their whole perceptual capacity, are invaded, engulfed by it. Their physical postures – the contorted face, fingers that grip so hard that the nails whiten, flinching tremulous limbs – all bear witness to the reality that they are suffering. What is happening is real, even if it has had to be set up in the most self-conscious, artificial way. The lashes of the whip may draw blood. This is something raw that no sophisticated intellect can defuse or deflate. The masochist, by both suffering and having his pain witnessed by the other person, is getting a strong sense of reality, a sense of animal vulnerability and of the harsh forces that oppose his longings.

Etsuko, obsessed with the young farm-hand Saburo, deliberately burns her hand so that the whole palm is blistered. Her motives are only hinted at, but later on she tells Saburo that she did it for him. He replies by comparing her to a beggar who tries to make him feel pity, and calls her a 'proud beggar'. Mishima notes that Saburo 'did not know it was Etsuko's pain that made her proud'.

Enduring any kind of ordeal gives the individual an opportunity both to taste the bitter unpalatable side of experience and to return refreshed. For some reason, human beings do not thrive when they are deprived of all challenge: they soften or harden up, become bored, irritable, lose their sense of humour, their vitality. Getting your own way once too often actually undermines the spirit, which enjoys the stimulus of facing new problems and learning the skills to overcome difficulties. There is even a physiological basis for this need to be challenged: for example, in some cultures, babies are bound up in swaddling clothes, not as some naïve English Victorian travellers thought, as an act of cruel barbarism, but because it is a good way to develop the infantile musculature, since the baby struggles hard against these bonds.

In adults, a sense of one's own limitations is equally important. Perhaps this is particularly so in more privileged mileux where one is often confronted by the importance of making the right choice. The necessity to choose from a number of alternatives – which career, which computer, which brand of extra-virgin olive oil – puts everyone in an imaginary position of omnipotence. One is expected to imagine a number of different possibilities, to disperse oneself over a range of choices, then to come down on one or two in particular. The idea of choice is one of the central tenets of capitalism, but in fact it is more of an annoyance than anything. It is usually a relief to find that one's choices are limited, perhaps because of having the wrong qualifications or a tight budget (I am not talking about people who are actually on or below the poverty line). It simplifies matters and again makes choosing more a matter of resourcefulness than lordly discrimination.

Bondage makes freedom seem worth having once again,

because freedom loses its definition unless it is set in some kind of contrast. When there is no restriction, freedom becomes simply the feeling of flailing around pointlessly, like a hapless astronaut in a bubble suit. Masochism involves a symbolic restriction of the body. At the most basic level, this creates a physical experience of opposition, between sensory deprivation and extending oneself freely in movement. But the meaning of bondage goes further. It expresses the fact that although one seems, perhaps, to be a free person, actually there are all kinds of invisible ties. Although there are no obvious reasons for suffering, one might still feel ill at ease in the world, or as the French say, *mal dans la peau*. In this position, persecuted by the sense of petty irritations but unsure whether they come from one's inner world or the environment outside, plagued by a sensitive conscience, one might long to put oneself to the test. The ordeal involved in a sexual submission cannot help but produce a sense of focus in the body, and this is important to combat the malaise that can result from an imaginative dispersal over an undefined terrain. And for all sorts of reasons, this is a problem which affects many people rather than just a few; the breaking-down of tight-knit communities, for example, leads to the types of interior malaise caused by a kind of vacant, floating freedom. The need is for definition, location. Masochism incarnates the need for a restraint that is enforced by an external force, not self-restraint. It incarnates needs that are a kind of cultural blind spot, because most enlightened thought tends to favour freedom from constraint. Masochism exposes the limit of such libertarian discourses by its seemingly contradictory presentation of the struggle between life and death. This struggle enhances vitality. What makes self-assertion wither away is the inability to find anything to struggle against, the retreat of prohibition.

The masochist handles suffering by embracing it for its salutary qualities. Though suffering is not in itself sexual, though it is an experience that feels bad rather than good, it can tip into extreme pleasure or can become the preliminary to that if treated by particular procedures. These involve trusting your own body, being in touch with the subtlety of bodily sensation, and allowing the sensation to slide from one coloration to the other.

The embracing of suffering for its salutary properties may well remind the reader of religious devotions involving the use of pain inflicted by oneself or others, ascetic practices such as self-flagellation. At the same time, it should be evident that there is an important difference. Religious self-mortification involves a wide array of practices – from the wearing of clothes that chafe the skin, fasting and celibacy to early rising – all designed to humble the flesh. Sexual mortification, on the other hand, has its rewards in this world and in erotic satisfactions that are out of bounds for religious devotees. The monk's asceticism is a permanent discipline, involving a community, whereas the masochist, who is only a member of the community of lovers, sets up an ordeal that is undergone relatively quickly. The monk has a religious belief that keeps him on the road to heaven, and the masochist does not; indeed, his behaviour would probably be considered as profane from a believer's perspective. But both monk and masochist are aware of the importance of integrating pain and privation into experience rather than denying it. Both have found their own way of translating a concern with mortality or negativity into a useful set of keys for living.

Although religious beliefs have lost a lot of ground, ascetic practices are on the increase, with the rise of body piercing, mortification of the appetite through vegetarian or other kinds of special diet, and pushing oneself to the limit through exercise. They may be begun in the effort to achieve a better figure, for example, but they quickly take on another kind of meaning. Everyone who has ever dieted knows that it is a sure way to become obsessionally interested in eating, because appetite when frustrated becomes a pressing force rather than just a mild prompt. Twenty lengths in a cold swimming-pool boost your internal circulation, but you have to overcome the horror of the initial contact to get moving at all. These kinds of self-punishment can remind you of the stuff you are made of, its frailty, its receptiveness, its necessary relationship to the outside world.

Physical suffering is even more important for the contemporary ascetic than for his religious antecedent because – and this may be hard to grasp in any abstract way – the only way to comprehend suffering is to go through it, to experience it, to represent it to oneself and to have it witnessed by another person. During the centuries when religious belief was widespread, suffering was, as is often sardonically remarked, considered good for the soul. Watching it all was God, a compassionate entity who valued the sacrifices, understood the difficulties of His adherents and prepared their plot in a better world. Everyone could afford Him.

Nowadays, if you want a witness to your suffering you probably have to go to a psychotherapist or psychoanalyst. They are a lot more expensive than God, and your suffering will speak in a different voice, will articulate its truth along different lines. It has no value in itself, it builds no credit in an other-wordly bank account, as it used to. The aim will be to diminish suffering, to make you more comfortable in yourself, less pathological. The means to this end is talking.

It seems to me small wonder that significant numbers of people prefer to take the ascetic road, integrating the necessity of pain into their lives, rather than the therapeutic one, by which they continually revisit their pathologies and disorders in an extended, one-sided and possibly dreary conversation. Yet people who tattoo or pierce their bodies are likely to be described as self-mutilating, people who fast as anorectic. The only form of asceticism that seems fully socially acceptable is exercise, though warnings abound that it should be done 'in moderation'. Such demands for moderation imply a life lived in tones of grey from beginning to end, the idea of living in the utmost timidity, in fear of the ecstatic potential of your own body, of your force and capacity for passion. If you were to live like this, life would lack vigour and scope for initiative, and become a constant nagging vigil against yourself. Life itself is exceptional, not moderate; to live moderately is to trivialize it and waste it. This is what contemporary ascetics know.

Masochism participates in asceticism, creatively reworks religious narratives into a new story of death and rebirth, allows a secular comprehension of categories that have almost vanished from the vocabulary: fatality, rapture. These terms are at the extreme ends of the spectrum. But then, erotic pain is all about extremity. Masochism, in its eccentric eroticism, makes explicit what most contemporary asceticism merely hints at: the affirmation of the body's frailty as a gateway to intense pleasure.

Good manners and social cohesion demand that we behave with reserve and consideration. In general, there is no reason to argue with this state of affairs. But the recurrent necessity to dampen down one's enthusiasms and emotional currents can lead to a feeling of atrophy. Impulses have to be mediated through a battery of self-censorship, which means that most fall by the wayside and never reach fruition. Nothing is ever initiated for fear of rocking the boat, and when you reach this point you may feel that life has become very dull and that you yourself have 'lost it'. That is, if you were ever aware of having it in the first place. In this state of mind, which for many people can continue for their whole lifetime, nothing ever happens. There is a lack of stories. The clichéd image of an elderly woman peeping out of her net curtains in the hope of seeing something worth gossiping about comes to mind. For her, the only stories are about other people, so she has to make the most of them.

This kind of atrophy, where no narrative is present, is fertile ground for the reception of narrative. Stories often take these stagnant moments as their starting point, in which the central character is introduced to the reader, leading a life that is remarkable only for its ordinariness. For example, the opening sentences of Joseph Conrad's novel *The Secret Agent*, could hardly be more humdrum: 'Mr Verloc, going out in the morning, left his shop nominally in charge of his brother-in-law. It could be done, because there was very little business at any time, and practically none before the evening.'

Yet this novel goes on to deal with paranoia, anarchy, insanity. The quiet frustration that occurs when time passes without event builds up a longing for some change in circumstance. This longing may be so strong that it does not matter whether things change for better or worse; anything seems better than a world without stimulus, a grey world. Novels and films often use this knowledge, helping the viewer or reader to form an initial identification with a central character who is eking out an existence just as dull as their own, and then setting change into motion.

I have already argued that the most popular storyline is probably that of 'boy meets girl'. But Christianity has been supplying us with quite a different storyline for the last two millennia.

The Christ story is one that gathers most of its intensity around the extensive torture, humiliation and public execution of a man who is the Son of God. Its narrative depiction in the form of the twelve stations of the cross is to be found on the walls of Roman Catholic churches. Each illustrates an individual scene of Christ's passion, such as the crowning with thorns, or the bearing of the cross, and they increase in pathos to the culminating point of the final crucifixion at Calvary.

We know that we enjoy identifying with a dynamic hero or heroine who overcomes the odds and triumphs over enemies, who ends up getting the girl or boy. But what is less admissible is how much pleasure and meaning is gained from identification with a body in pain. Christ is always worshipped as a figure nailed to a cross, bleeding and mutilated, scorned and betrayed. This is also a cherished, though generally secret, vision of ourselves.

Some part of us gets an intense pleasure from the sense of being 'infinitely ravaged', as Michel Leiris puts it. It is partly the aesthetic sense that responds strongly to representations of pain. The suffering, tragic, mortal body is made exquisitely beautiful by its proximity to death. Although one admires the dynamic, entrepreneurial hero, the passive vulnerable victim evokes a more felt response. The hero represents the ideal, but the tragic victim, the Christ, exalts and beautifies one's own suffering.

This may be one of the reasons why, in Catholic churches at least, there is a strong emphasis on the aesthetic elements of the Church and the Mass: incense, candles, flowing robes, ritual gestures, paintings and statues. The congregation needs unconsciously to develop an appreciation of the sublime in order to make use of the Christ narrative for its own purposes. Without that skill, one is left to an unrelieved and perhaps unremitting sense of self-pity that is likely to turn to cankerous resentment, the martyr complex.

If Christians do have a masochistic identification with the suffering Christ, this same possibility presents itself in other ways for non-believers. Tragedy in the theatre or opera can fulfil this need for a projection on to a figure of tortured innocence. One difference is that figures like Shakespeare's Lear or Benjamin Britten's Peter Grimes are shown to have some character flaw that brings about their downfall. More truly Christlike is the persecuted gunman in Westerns, for example Clint

Eastwood in *The Outlaw Josey Wales*. This film shows the hero founding and protecting, against the odds, a kind of alternative multiracial community, before fading out to the blood-drips of his final, fatal injury. Clint's tough demeanour is hardly skin deep: he is really a kind of saint. The sad, exiled cowboys and sharpshooters of Westerns contrast with the genuinely grisly protagonists of gangster films, whom we are not meant to like in the same way. Al Pacino's sneering physiognomy has quite a different popular appeal: he is never expected to perform acts of self-sacrifice or even heroism, just to act like a tough guy. The gangster learns nothing from suffering, but he has to win first time or take the rap; audience pity tends not to be aroused. The enjoyable elements are raw energy, plenty of movement, and a fantasized escape from feminine restriction.

Watching the good guy being attacked by his enemies – Cary Grant running pointlessly in the open fields as he is bombarded by a low-flying aeroplane in Alfred Hitchcock's *North by Northwest* – is far more viscerally gripping. Identificatory masochism happens in those sections of films (or plays or books) where we see the hero being unfairly beaten up by a gang of hoodlums. Or when we gain a distinct pleasure from seeing Juliette Binoche's beauty simultaneously ruined and enhanced by multiple facial bruising after the car accident at the beginning of Krzysztof Kieslowski's film *Three Colours Blue*. Of course, part of this kind of pleasure involves a tension about whether the character will overcome this humiliating episode and find in himself or herself the qualities necessary to succeed. But the reader or viewer gets something very important out of the depiction of the downside, even if this seems to be written out by the solution of the ending.

When it comes to the masochistic sexual encounter, things are a little different. The binding, flagellation and humiliation of the masochist follow fairly closely the classic New Testament narrative, but in what amounts to parody rather than sincere imitation. (Not that there is any malice involved, or even any conscious reference. The Christ story is a pervasive motif in a post-Christian culture, and it is this motif that is grasped at some level as a means through which to enact suffering and pleasure.) Where Christ's mortification ended in his death, the masochist's ends in orgasmic satisfaction. The masochist may need the endurance of an ascetic, but he is too much of a hedonist or supersensualist to leave things at that stage. He pushes things further, by staging the self-annihilation that the ascetic only suggests.

Masochism embraces pain and undergoes its full onslaught in order to come out fresh on the other side, in a narrative of extremes which moves from hell to heaven, from Good Friday to Easter. Clearly, it holds some important messages about how suffering can be used.

Redemptive Endings

Masochism shares with religious discourses the ability to make use of suffering, to describe or redescribe it as a valuable aspect of life. What is essential to this understanding of suffering is that it should be set in a story *in which it is not the last thing that happens*. It has to be followed by an upbeat ending. Christ is crucified, but he rises from the dead. Without the redemption, his previous tortures would have been futile, and the only message that one could take from this would be a depressing one: that man's inhumanity to man is an unavoidable fact of life. This is something that one very much does not want to think.

French anthropologist René Girard has addressed the issue of inhumanity in much of his work, and argues that such is the level of aggression in any community that legal systems and other kinds of checks and balances are essential to prevent serious outbreaks such as murder and warfare. But the need to express murderous wishes, what he calls 'mimetic violence', is so strong that from time to time a scapegoat is chosen, generally either from outside the community – a stranger – or from the ranks of those who are least protected by family structures, such as orphans. The scapegoat is bound, loaded with blame for the sins of the whole community, abused, tortured and ritually murdered. The process is a happy one for the community, which emerges refreshed and unified by its collusive killing. This kind of theory owes much of its persuasive quality to the fact that it is prepared to think the unthinkable: that as individuals we are all potentially murderous, and that those who are victimized share no particular virtue or vice but are simply the ones who have been denied society's protection.

Something like Girard's thinking seems to inform Robert Altman's fascinating film *Short Cuts*, a portrait of Los Angeles as a vicious, immoral community. All levels of society are represented in the film, including an alcoholic night-club singer who neglects her daughter, a cop who is cheating on his wife, and a callous businessman. The inability to face aggression against each other results in death for those others who are vulnerable in some way: the little boy run over by a waitress who cannot face the truth about her abusive boyfriend, the daughter who commits suicide, the girl murdered by a sexually frustrated swimming-pool attendant. It is as if something evil is present that must find an outlet in violence, to the relief of all of the characters, even the most caring among them. As in Girard's theory, there are no good guys or bad guys, just a society that demands human sacrifices and gets them from its least protected members.

Girard, a Catholic, considers Christ's passion an exception to the rule of the scapegoat. The Christian narrative is not one of temporary social cohesion effected by communal violence against a defenceless innocent, but an ordeal deliberately undergone in order to save a whole world from its own internal corruption. Though there are striking similarities to the sacrifice of the scapegoat, there are also important differences.

One difference is that neither the scapegoat nor the murderous society is redeemed by the human sacrifice; all that results is a temporary sense of relief, a lull in hostilities, a short-lived sense of unity and cohesion. Where Christ's passion is sublime, capable of uplifting his adherents and making them transcend their differences, the characters in the Altman film who do have some compassion are diminished in stature by what happens. Far from being redeemed, they are in some sense morally damned by a mutual solidarity that involves participating in a sneaky kind of generalized cynicism.

Masochism can be interpreted as deploying aspects of both the scapegoat scenario and the Christian one. If one believes, with Girard and many others, that violence is an ever-present force, surging around and through everyone, masochism could be seen as a contrary way of confronting it. By making oneself the focus for a controlled version of that violence, one for a moment grasps it physically, lives through it, acts as an escape route for it. The masochist plugs into the electric current of social rage to combine its crackling spark with his or her own eroticism.

The combination with sexual pleasure as the final outcome makes that pain possible. And it can be argued that Christians also gain extreme pleasure from the projection of themselves on to the figure of the suffering Christ – although it is not straight erotic enjoyment but a sublimated, enraptured kind of joy.

The masochist, by contrast, gets his or her thrills in a carnal, profane way. The encounter ends not with apotheosis, but orgasm. The story is about spending rather than saving. If the world is a violent, mean and sordid place, the masochist rejects transcendence as a way of handling it. The only way out is through.

Rapture

Spirituality and sexuality are both liberators of the soul, and both are surprisingly democratic. This is in the obvious sense that everyone can walk into a candlelit church, and few people are so unattractive as to lack for sexual contact. Both versions of masochism – the transcendent kind and the worldly kind, the sacred and the profane, are adept at the discipline of transforming pain and suffering into something useful, enjoyable or meaningful – in the first case for the purposes of spiritual rapture, in the second for supersensual purposes.

Religious sublimation and the sexual impulse are often surprisingly intertwined. Take, for example, this stanza from a seventeenth-century poem by George Herbert, 'The Agonie':

> Who knows not Love, let him assay
> And taste that juice, which on the cross a pike
> Did set again abroach; then let him say
> If ever he did taste the like.
> Love is that liquor sweet and most divine,
> Which my God feels as bloud; but I, as wine.

The bleeding Christ figure is being savoured – even recommended to others who do not know his particular qualities – as a kind of divine drink, in this vampiric metaphor. The uncanny thing is that somehow the poem underlines the agony of Christ in a kind of whisper which accompanies the supposed enjoyment of him. The 'juice' that is flowing is his blood – Christ is endlessly, infinitely ravished, perpetually in agony.

The agony and the ecstasy are bound together. The raptures of St Teresa of Avila are another example. In her *Life*, she attempts a description of her mystical experiences (which would often take her unawares at peculiarly embarrassing moments, to the point where she began praying that the Lord would stop favouring her in this way): 'In these raptures the soul no longer seems to animate the body . . . often it comes like a strong, swift impulse, before your thought can forewarn you of it or you can do anything to help yourself; you see and feel this cloud, or this powerful eagle, rising and bearing you up with it on its wings.'

The Bernini statues of St Teresa in ecstasy have been much commented on for their representation of what seems like a woman in the spasm of a sexual climax. But mysticism is a specific experience and should not be confused with orgasm. What is remarkable about her own description is its innocence. 'When I tried to resist these raptures, it seemed that I was being lifted up by a force beneath my feet so powerful that I know nothing to which I can compare it, for it came with a much greater vehemence than any other spiritual experience and I felt as if I were being ground to powder.'

The sense of being overwhelmed to the point of atomization that St Teresa felt, or the euphoric, enraptured feeding that Herbert evokes in his poem about the dying Christ, bear witness to a fundamental capacity for being overwhelmed. I have already drawn on Leo Bersani's crucial rewriting of theories of sexuality, in which he shows how this enjoyment of being ruptured by something external is the essence of eroticism. Eroticism involves the sense of an interior self, a self that is always vulnerable to invasion from the outside – that defends itself yet longs for the invasion. Masochism lends itself to all erotic experience in this sense, since it involves the capacity to be shattered into joy or *jouissance* by an extreme pleasure that is also intense suffering. And the transcendental versions of rapture are an indication that 'eroticism' is a broad category, which covers much more than genital sexuality.

Religious or inner experience does not normally end in orgasm, and this is not the only difference from sexual masochism. These two instances of eroticism vary enormously in their relation to irony. The contemporary prevalence of kitsch and parody offers a good context for subcultural sado-masochism, which skilfully deploys ironic techniques to create its outlandish scenarios. But times are hard for the mystics, the visionaries, who nowadays seem to be left with the choice of becoming artists, going mad, or both. Both mystics and masochists, however, draw on the common source of masochism, where painful pleasure is so great that identity breaks down in the feeling of being flooded by joy. At the point of rapture, no irony, no self-protective self-consciousness, can be preserved any longer.

Ritual Transgressions

In this concluding chapter I have looked at what wider messages masochism has within it. In particular I have linked the religious or mystical experience and the sexual variety, showing that ultimately they both represent erotic experience, though they come out differently.

Why do some people become masochistic in an obvious way, while others do not? In many of the writers and thinkers I have quoted over the course of this book, I would detect a particular quality that perhaps does make them a distinct group: they share a quality of intensity, a kind of fervour. Perhaps it is this inner force that demands to be registered, that refuses to be dampened down, that makes them stand out. As Theodor Reik says, the masochist cannot be broken from the outside. Every endurance of pain, humiliation or suffering only goes to increase this resilience.

Their fervour means that those people who could be identified as masochistic tend to be imaginative risk-takers, people who need to know what it is like in the world outside. Another way of putting this might be that being intensely sexual by definition (as masochism implies) also means displaying strong levels of curiosity. The desire is not for mastery of the world, or for power in it, but for enveloping, taking in the external, especially its unknown and unfamiliar aspects. This voluptuous curiosity looks for fresh encounters, and is unlikely to be satisfied with the kind of knowledge that can be gained through culture. The transgressive need of the masochist makes risk-taking and direct exposure to the unknown an important part of his or her life. When you deliberately get lost in a foreign city late at night, refusing directions to the nearest metro station, you are taking this kind of risk. When you let a stranger into your house you are doing the same thing. These risks involve real danger, as if you have to expose yourself in that way to get any real new knowledge.

French philosopher Simone Weil may seem at first glance an unlikely candidate for the category of the masochistic adventurer. She and Simone de Beauvoir were the first women admitted to the Ecole Normale Supérieure in Paris to study philosophy, and she became a Marxist through identifying with the sufferings of the working class. Her difference from most intellectuals of her cadre was that she chose to live this out, by taking on dangerous and dismal shifts in a steel factory, where she learnt that proletarian labour was even more soul destroying than she had suspected. From these kinds of experiences (she also did agrarian work) she developed a unique vision of a non-materialist socialism that she elaborated in her works of philosophy. De Gaulle thought her mad for her proposal of front-line nursing squads during the war; George Steiner has repeatedly described her life as 'pathological'. She died of consumption at the age of thirty-four, in England.

From a conventional perspective, people like Weil make no

sense. The words 'self-destructive' and 'suicidal' are undoubtedly accurate in describing the repeated way in which she jeopardized her health and well-being and put her fragile, emaciated body at risk. Yet she was exceptional for her brilliance, vision and courage. The word that really captures her quality is 'heart-breaking'. If one imaginatively – passionately rather than coldly – engages with her life and ideas, they are very moving and powerful.

An appreciation of masochism opens up another way of understanding Simone Weil and other latter-day saints. Weil's thought was intensely masochistic, identifying with the agonies of Christ and wanting to resemble him. It is as if she brought all her painful experience into an interior self that was a great open wound or exposed heart, accepting of everything.

These kinds of lives are lived in the shadow of mortality. They defy the basic laws of survival by their love affair with their own extinction. They are not miserable lives for that, however, but eventful, adventurous, lived to the hilt. This is in contrast with most of us, who tend to eke out longer existences with fewer high points. It is part of an intense curiosity to nurture the thought, 'Since that is where I'm going, why shouldn't I try to glimpse what it's like in advance?' – as if the thought of death could be lived alongside one's life, life seen as a journey towards death rather than a span of vitality.

Of course, that made perfect sense in a religious perspective, when one believed in Heaven as a place for which one had to earn a certain number of qualifying points while stuck down here, in a kind of parole system. But it is odd that the notion should persist within masochism in a secular society. What sense can be made of it?

The sense of fatality could be understood as a kind of innate knowledge, built into the psyche. This point is essentialist, and there can be no apologies for that. Here is a rather repellent metaphor that explains something of what I am trying to get over. When a human baby is born, in its intestines is lodged a microscopic species that continues to accompany him or her throughout life. Upon the person's death, these creatures finally flourish and are the agents by which the body is broken down – literally, the worms that eat it. In a biological way, we carry our deaths around with us. My point is that this is not merely biological.

By getting down into the dirt, whether it is the masochistic client cleaning the prostitute's stilettos or Simone Weil working alongside the proletarians in a steel foundry, one gets a foretaste of mortality.

We are a long way now from the sense of masochism as playful, humorous, poetic or amorous, or from its capacity to redeem. I have moved back to look at that moment somewhere in the middle of the sado-masochistic act when the pain really is unbearable and authentically deadly. To undergo this, there has to be enormous self-discipline.

A vision of death is acted out, death imagined in two ways. First, as an inevitable event that will happen in the future. Second, as all the ways in which it presents itself during life, all the forms of morbidity from which people suffer. The achievement of the masochist is to attempt to grasp, with the imagination, to suffer passively, with the body and will, the transition between life and death.

The person who submits voluntarily to pain must, as I have said, be the dauntless kind, and the reason for this is the amount of formidable forces he or she conjures up in the course of submission – because there has to be a moment of seriousness, when the seductive comedy, the dressing-up and the exaggerated postures are over, and before the pain has been transformed or relieved by erotic enjoyment. All the risk of masochism lies in that moment. It is a silent moment, because one of temporary self-extinction.

What does this concern about death, this wish to get to

know it in advance, imply? To try to establish that, I want to contrast this concern with the usual idea one has of the relationship between life and death. The normal view would be that if life is a sentence, death comes as a full stop. If in life you run forward, with death you go over the edge of a cliff, like one of those Walt Disney characters who cycles in the air in puzzlement for a moment or two before dropping like a stone.

The alternative view is the fairly familiar one that in the midst of life we are in death. But that does not just imply that we gradually lose our loved ones, or that our own death is always a possibility. The ramifications go further. It could be put simply as the idea that morbidity and vitality are the two forces that impel everyone through life. Morbidity is present in all sorts of ways: illness, madness, unhappiness, addiction. Freud came to believe that the death instinct was stronger even than the desire for self-preservation, and he was sensitive to the fact that people will do a lot to preserve the morbidity in their lives. Freud's psychoanalysis was aimed at restructuring unhappiness, evening it out, rather than effecting a cure.

What I am *not* going to argue is that all these forms of morbidity are simply necessary. There is a logic here: all of the four categories that I have listed above are universal and there has never been a time when any of them disappeared. Man is a sick animal. In moderate societies like ours, there is still plenty of casual violence, the hospitals are still overcrowded, and people who are hale and hearty find leisure outlets for the sick sides of themselves in blood-and-gore films like *Pulp Fiction*. Quentin Tarantino's film neutralizes the emotions by its fast pace and its jokiness, so that you can watch someone's brains splatter across a car seat in cheerful equanimity. This technique allows the material to bounce away from the mind, so that what you have seen is a speeded-up boys' comic.

Although I want to say that death, as consciousness and as symptom and as fascination, is ever-present in people, I do not

155

want to leave it at that or imply that nothing can be done on the side of life. As I have tried to show, masochism always returns to life after the painful ordeal, and the witnessing of the ordeal by the torturer means that there is never a moment of absolute abandonment. The sexual submission happens between two people, within the bounds of the contract, so however unbearable the moment of pain may seem, the masochist always remains connected. The sense of absolute despair or of being abandoned is avoided by these advance manipulations.

One of the messages of masochism is that one should do one's suffering in company, rather than being alone with it. The enemy is not suffering, but disconnectedness – including the kind of cynicism that involves the decision to cut oneself off from contact. Pain in itself is a relative experience, which can be made worse or better by the context. When I visit my acupuncturist, who is also a good friend whom I have known for over a decade, the pain of the needles during treatment may be intense, but because of her presence I find it quite bearable. It is when pain is depersonalized, when it does not belong, that it is most desperate. Some clinical traditions actually empha- size this depersonalization, for example, by the wearing of white coats or other uniforms, the use of a dog-Latin vocabu- lary and the treating of the patient as a collection of symptoms.

Death may be what the masochist wants to glimpse, but from a place of safety, from within the protection of an erotic bond, a partnership. In a relationship, you can go almost any- where, right through the circles of hell and purgatory, as Dante did with Virgil. (Even the client has some sort of partnership with the prostitute, if only a mercantile one.) The sense of being linked to another person even right inside the eye of the storm is what allows the masochist to make the adventure. He could only do it knowing how much life he had in him, and how much to go back to afterwards.

The Martyr and the Masochist

In *Venus in Furs*, Severin relates how the stories of the Christian martyrs filled him with a mixture of horror and fascination. Yet the extreme torments of these saints bear little relation to the playful scenarios he comes to contrive with his willing accomplice, Wanda. Saintly suffering has been inherited by today's world as the martyr complex or attitude.

Nowadays, the term 'martyr' is used sardonically. Obviously it no longer applies to anyone who suffers and dies for their Christian beliefs. The term has come to indicate the kind of person who radiates a sense of moral superiority, and a suppressed resentment that emerges glorified as an idealism which reproves and condemns the inadequacies of lesser beings.

This is a personality type and a current of behaviour, one which can in particular historical moments become powerful and dangerous, expecially in politics. For example, the massacres of the Khmer Rouge in Cambodia seem to have been driven by a genuine idealism. The moral martyr will proclaim how few hours they sleep each night, so that everyone knows how hard they are working. At the logical extreme, they are totalitarian. The denunciation is the key strategy of resentful idealists, who see appalling shortcomings everywhere around them, except in themselves. Such people are recognizable by their accusatory tone of voice, by their tendency to find fault in others, by an aggression denied and projected on to others, and by a glint in their eye. They may be seen as charismatic in that they appeal to, and mobilize, a generalized resentment that will not speak its name.

As a character type, the modern martyr is quite distinct from the masochist. Nor is he or she a sadist; this self-righteous idealist is quite another species than Sade's libertines, who at the very least take a direct pleasure in their atrocities.

157

The discourse of the modern martyr is not one of rampant egoistic lust, of an appetite that swallows up everything in its path, but of an uptight cruelty that denies its own involvement in pleasure. Thus when the Nazis were tried for their crimes, they refused to speak in a human way, merely citing bureaucratic documents and instructions, as if they were without any kind of reflexiveness, any capacity to comprehend their own motivations. There may be sadism here, but it is so suppressed as to be almost unrecognizable as any kind of pleasure.

Persecutory idealists represent themselves as singular, absolute and zealous, projecting a ready-made myth of the strong, strict father who will protect the good and persecute the sinners. Using a set of drastically over-simplified symbolizations, such people divide the world up into the unattainably good, strong and powerful (which is to be fanatically subscribed to) and the irredeemably bad, poisonous and alien (which is to be cleansed away, crushed by the wrath of God, etc.).

Part of the attraction of the moral martyr is this simplicity, which finds echoes in all of us at different times, and especially at difficult times. Idealism of this kind means losing touch with what you have worked out as your own *modus operandi*, your own sense of what is right, and instead allowing yourself to become a ventriloquist's dummy.

Not only are they different, but the martyr and the masochist are natural enemies. Masochism uses suffering to explore and create, moving through it to the other side. But moral martyrdom clutches on to suffering, neither fully experiencing its bite nor ever letting it go into pleasure. It becomes a chronic ache that is carried around and set into currency, a resentful, generalized misery.

I have talked about masochism both as a sexual phenomenon and as an artistic or mystical aspiration. In both cases there is an enquiry into the nature of life and death, the two forces that accompany everyone for their span on earth. Masochism tends to the sublime, however wretched and sordid its initial moves and gestures may be. The wretched and the sordid are in fact essential to the attainment of the sublime, because, in a phrase I have used several times in this book, masochism is all about getting down into the dirt. Masochism is a movement which integrates the lowest impulses with the highest; it is a story about falling in order to ascend.

Moral martyrdom, on the other hand, aims at a standard of purity that excludes human fault. Where masochism includes the most rancid detritus in its scope, making all this unwelcome matter into the tissue of pleasure, moral martyrdom excludes, purifies, hacks away at the roots of what it is to be human. To be human is to want contact, including sexual contact. But a desexualized idealism distances the individual from the human community. By projecting oneself upon a dead ideal of authority, one becomes cut off from life and ready to reduce the lives of others. Thus Margaret Thatcher's act as education minister of stopping the daily free bottle of milk that used to go to schoolchildren, cutting off the cheering flow of life, of maternal warmth, of basic human nourishment.

I have given one answer as to why this position is such a popular one: because people who are under particular and perhaps chronic pressure may become disoriented to the point of fixing on to simple, authoritarian strictures that bear no relation to their own human needs. The result is disaster, because such ideals actively attack the human impulses towards love, sharing and community through paranoid exclusion (for example, race hate), moral censoriousness and the adulation of models of perfection.

With the moral martyr, something is going wrong. It is the same thing that goes wrong with everyone, and maybe most of us fall into this category at least some of the time. After all, the widespread notions of moderation and prudence do nothing to help us recognize the need for self-renewal through enlivening, invigorating self-rupture. These prevailing repressions perhaps strengthen society, but de-energize the individuals in it.

Moral martyrdom can be a mood, a feeling, a tempting position to assume, for example during an argument: 'I gave you the best years of my life'; 'I've been through hell for your sake'; 'You've never even tried to understand me'. It is the guilt trip, the hard-done-by position, it comes out under stress, when you are tired, your relationship at breaking point, and irritation combusts into mutual reproaches, as melodramatic as they are self-pitying. At such moments one is dimly aware (through the blanket of annoyance and self-pity) of being at a low ebb, unable to do anything better than circle around in this negative field, piling on the anguish. It is a compulsion to misery that most of us have gone through from time to time, last year, last weekend.

Masochism is at the opposite extreme. Masochists are pluralist, and have a largeness of spirit, an expansiveness. They can easily project themselves outwards and empathize with others, though they may sometimes want to protect themselves from their own susceptibility. Where idealists listen to the external voice of authority, masochists are thoroughly populated, have a choir (or a rabble) of inner voices. Masochists are always moving out of themselves with a mixture of curiosity and intense pleasure in enveloping a fresh version of the world.

What messages could masochism offer on a political and cultural level? The necessity to represent millions of people makes the political machine quite incapable of the sensitive responsiveness that is one of masochism's hallmarks. The discourse of politics is often paranoid; it is desexualized and impersonal in its processes.

If politics provides only an ersatz witness to human suffering, is there any other place for the masochistic impulse to be felt, outside of erotic and artistic engagement? Could one, at any rate, elaborate the kind of ethical outlook that masochism has to offer, at whatever level?

First of all, bondage. The masochistic perspective asserts the importance of being bound. For example, privilege always reasserts itself historically, and there is no reason to think this will change, possibly less so now than ever, since the utopian socialist ideals of the post-war period are well and truly annihilated. Privilege is quite indefensible; but since it may be ineradicable, it should be accompanied by a distinct sense of obligation, a will to return to the poor and disadvantaged some of the goods that one is unfairly enjoying. The newly revived culture of philanthropic giving in the US is one sign of this beginning to happen. Bondage on the ethical level means a commitment, allowing oneself to be tied to something or someone. It means being bound to one's word, or bound to make good a promise. Bondage is an appreciation that restriction is not something negative in itself, that freedom from restraint leads to nothing but empty space.

The other, more positive word for bondage is attachment. You are attached to your lover, your family, your city. You are also attached to particular childhood memories, to a song by Van Morrison, to vanilla-chocolate-fudge ice-cream, to your own ideas and opinions. Attachment is more than affection, it is a way of patterning individuality. One of the most endearing things one can discover in another person is a shared attachment. Often this is how friendships and love affairs begin, and why they endure. From one attachment springs another.

But bondage is also a sharp, cutting term: the leather thongs that bind you also chafe the skin, or force you to assume an uncomfortable position. The sense of attachment is indissoluble from the sense of restriction, of being put upon by obligations and commitments. Bondage is a reminder that every choice is a diminishing of the range of possibilities. It is a physical exemplification of the sense of being frustrated by one's constraints. Bondage is not much fun if there is nobody around to untie you, and the whole point of masochistic bondage is that your lover *is* going to let you go – eventually. In the meantime, you are at their mercy. You had better trust them before you start things going in the first place. Letting somebody tie you up means you trust them. Likewise, though commitment and obligation reduce autonomy, they develop the kind of interpersonal risk that trust necessitates.

If bondage emphasizes trust and obligation, what about the middle phase of the masochistic encounter, the ordeal of punishment? Suppose one thinks of punishment as something that takes place on a level that seems genuinely beyond human reach. For example, there have been moments in my life when everything went wrong at once, when the downward spiral seemed unending. (This seems to be a common experience. When everything goes right at once, one seems to be quite blithe about it; it never comes into question and seems perfectly natural.) At times like that, it is easy to feel that you are being punished by the Fates, pursued by a run of bad luck, jinxed. Just as the stock market periodically crashes, so does your life.

Under the whip, the masochist may scream and cry and thrash about hopelessly. And the same kind of thing happens, pretty much, when life goes awry. You complain, you manoeuvre futilely, you make things worse for yourself. There is no good way of getting through. But it is a catharsis. By the time it is over all your rage, resentment and self-disgust are out. What replaces the bad blood is new blood. Like St Sebastian, who is the more filled with love the deeper he is pierced with arrows, the masochist saturates the channels created by pain with a renewed capacity for passion.

Punishment is the part that feels entirely negative at the time, but that is a prerequisite for the painful rupture taking place.

The tearing pain is necessary for what is to come. Taking one's punishment can be paraphrased as grasping the nettle. When things in life crash, it is usually because some limit has been reached, some developmental process needs to be faced, or because change is on the agenda. Being punished is what happens every time someone grows up, splits up with a lover, runs the London Marathon or gives birth. I have already shown how, in the autobiographical novels of Michel Leiris and Marguerite Duras, masochistic situations are undergone in order to transform emotional difficulties and distress into something that can be lived with. The ordeal builds fortitude, love and sanity in the person who is prepared to go into it.

Finally, there is the moment of sublime joy that compensates for everything the masochist has suffered. You have gone through the valley of death and emerged relatively unscathed. Your aching body longs for nothing so much as the release of erotic contact, the sublime – like a rocket going into space, a dramatic ascension that makes the whole thing worthwhile – a spasm, a convulsion, a shock of intense, absolute bliss.

This point makes sense of the whole of life's journey. In this flash of voluptuous insight, your wounds are healed, through sexual healing, carnal knowledge or the mystic's vision. You are not yourself, you do not know where you are or what you are doing; for that moment, there is a loss of consciousness. The body is flooded with sensation to the point of being nothing but feeling; losing its solidity and opacity, it becomes a live current of energy, a lightning conductor.

Release into the sublime is rebirth. Of course, you are the same old self, but with the batteries recharged and ready to fire (the bodywork, on the other hand, may look a little tatty). Rebirth is one of the things that people often sense they need, but they do not know how to go about achieving it (hence the success of evangelical Christian sects, which capitalize on this need and manipulate it for the purposes of mass conversions).

Periodically, things either go wrong or become stale and only through some process of challenge and renewal can the husk of the old be clawed off and the living body become energized enough to face the future. The sublime moment temporarily abolishes identity and allows it to come back as something fluid and responsive. Blissful rapture is a participation in something bigger than oneself, a recognition of God's grandeur. Masochism's final, unexpected message is to forget yourself – a difficult discipline.

A Notebook

I was looking for a notebook in which to write the ending of this essay. My lover passed me one with a buff cover, saying, 'You could use this.' As he knew, it was not an empty notebook waiting to be filled, but had within its blue-lined pages details of certain agreements made between myself and him.

These agreements or short-term contracts are, of course, a secret between the two of us. I am not intending to follow the example of Wanda von Sacher-Masoch, who rather disgracefully revealed the precise contents of that couple's agreement (though at least it was not until long after their life together was over).

So I cannot tell you what that slim notebook contains, just that rereading it was enough to make me smile and blush – which was perhaps what he intended.